3-Step Parenting

How to Replace Misbehavior with Cooperation

Richard O'Keef

© Copyright 2019 by Richard O'Keef

All rights reserved.

No part of this book may be reproduced, stored in a retrieval system, or transmitted in any form or by any means – electronic, mechanical, photocopy, recording, scanning, or other – except for brief quotations in critical reviews or articles, without prior written permission of the author.

Disclaimer: The reader must act responsibly and at his or her own risk when following the recommendations contained herein. The author shall have neither liability nor responsibility to any person or entity for harm or injury of person or property caused by any person in attempting to use the information in this book.

Front Cover Metaphor: Imagine you are in the forest pictured on the front cover. Can you hear the birds singing? Smell the crisp, clean air with that faint scent of pine? Feel the serenity? This picture symbolizes the calmness and peace of mind that 3-Step Parenting can give you. The Dad with his children represents the act of building relationships. And the Mom? She's behind the camera taking an Instagram-worthy photo.

ISBN 978-0-9787884-2-1

Contact: 3stepparenting@gmail.com
Website/Blog: 3stepparenting.com

Contents

1 Introduction 1

2 The Four Emotional Needs 11

3 The 3-Step Parenting Formula 19

Section 1 Build a Strong Relationship with your Children 25

4 Principle 1: Spend One-On-One Time with Each Child 27

5 Principle 2: Spend Family Time Together 37

6 Principle 3: Acknowledge Negative Feelings 55

7 Principle 4: Get to Know Your Kids 71

8 Principle 5: Make Positive Deposits 77

Section 2 Teach Children Life Skills, Good Values, and Desirable Behavior 83

9 Teach Life Skills 85

10 Teach Good Values 109

11 Teach Desirable Behavior 141

12 Model Good Behavior 149

13 Give Attention to Good Behavior 153

14 Offer Choices 161

Section 3 Skillfully Correct Children when their Behavior is Displeasing 165

15 Nine Practices that Undermine Progress 169

16 Start with These Skills	177
17 Ignore Annoying Behavior	187
18 When-Then Statements	191
19 Sibling Rivalry	197
20 Problem-Solve Together	205
21 Consequences	217
22 Tantrums	231
23 Seek Divine Guidance	235
Moving Forward	239
About the Author	241
Notes	245
Recommended Books	247

1

Introduction

If you are a parent (or in a parenting role), there is a set of procedures you can follow that will increase your children's desire to cooperate. This set of procedures is called *The 3-Step Parenting Formula*. It will help you put a stop to nearly every form of misbehavior. This formula will enable you to confidently replace your children's misbehavior with cooperation. When you learn how to be a 3-Step Parent, you will never wonder what to do again.

Is reminding, threatening and screaming your current strategy to get your child to do what you ask? See if this sounds familiar.

You make a request:

"Honey, it's time to get ready for bed."

You think maybe this time things will be different and she'll stop what she's doing, go brush her teeth, put on her jammies, give you a hug, turn out her light and get into bed. Hey, it could happen. But when you return you discover that she hasn't moved.

You *remind* her:

"Stop playing and get ready for bed."

"Okay," she says.

You know she knows her answer will appease you for a while and buy her some time. A few minutes later you look in on her.

Nothing.

You resort to your next level of persuasion: *threating*.

"If you don't get moving right now, you can forget about seeing friends this weekend. And I mean it."

"Okaaay," she says with more drama in her voice as if to imply, "Stop bugging me."

You try to suppress the thought that you have never followed through on that threat.

You know she hasn't paid any attention to you because this has been the routine for a long time: you ask, you remind, you threaten, and she does nothing.

You can feel the anger building up.

"How can she be so disrespectful; so disobedient – after all I do for her?"

The volcano inside you is about to erupt. She knows it, but she doesn't care. She's expecting you to explode because it's what usually happens. Finally, you've had enough and you *scream*: "How many times do I have to tell you? Get ready for bed! NOW! GO! MOVE!"

Finally, she starts to move. You hate to scream, but it seems to be the only way you can get her to obey. You feel guilty that you have to resort to such tactics, and frustrated that you don't know a better way.

That's just one of many scenarios that play out during the week which involve similar routines: Get in the car. Come for dinner. Get this room cleaned up – and the battles that follow.

Too often you are faced with annoying behaviors; behaviors that make you feel irritated and cause you to either give in to your child's demands or blow up. These behaviors include whining, clinging, teasing, dawdling, acting helpless, interrupting, tantrums, and bedtime battles.

Then there are the behaviors that make you feel provoked, challenged and angry; behaviors that produce power struggles such as ignoring, being defiant, saying "No," fighting with siblings, back-talking and doing the opposite of what you ask or demand.

You might be dealing with a child that seems to be out for revenge. They inflict physical damage, emotional hurt, use profanity and do horrible things that seem cold and calculated; things that cause you to think, *"How could you do this to me?"*

In such instances, you might catch yourself thinking, *"Where's the fun? This isn't what I signed up for. I thought parenting was supposed to be this rewarding experience and all I feel is frazzled."*

I have some good news. You are going to learn how to effectively take care of problem behavior, how to become unfrazzled, and how to put the fun into raising children. Imagine asking your child to get ready for bed **and she does it.** Or even better, she does it without being asked. Or how about asking her to get in the car, come for dinner, get this room cleaned up, and she starts to move on the first request? She obeys because she wants to. She does what you ask because she wants to please you. She doesn't want to let you down.

Sure, there will be times when she does not comply. When that happens, you will know what to do to effectively and lovingly correct her behavior without nagging, threatening or screaming. You are going to learn how to prevent most misbehavior from even happening, as well as find guidance on what to do when correction becomes necessary. No longer will you feel unprepared or have self-doubts. You will never have to wonder what to do again.

Parenting does not have to make you feel inadequate or incompetent.

You're probably thinking to yourself, *"Who is this guy to be giving me parenting advice?"*

I'm the father of six children – all adults now. But there was a time when I was in the trenches feeling pretty clueless. When I was a young parent I thought that love, common sense and intuition were all I needed to be a good parent. Then I found myself face to face with little people who were experts at whining, ignoring, interrupting, power struggles, temper tantrums, refusing to obey, doing the opposite, even out-right defiance. I loved my children with all my heart, but I wanted to control them and make them mind.

I tried using logic: "How would you like it if someone did that you?"

I tried enforcing good behavior: "Now say you're sorry and don't do it again."

I did the reminding, nagging, threatening and screaming. I remember saying on various occasions, "I'm sorry I screamed, but it was the only way I could get you to move." I spanked and I pinched. I counted to three and I put kids in timeout. My tactics seemed to work for a short time but misbehavior always returned.

I did what I did because **I didn't know any other way.** I was bewildered. I felt inadequate and unprepared.

Then one day when I was feeling particularly discouraged, I said, "Enough is enough. Parenting should not have to be this hard. There must be a better way."

So I bought books and attended lectures. I also listened to cassette tapes – it's true, I've been around *that* long. Up to this time I did not care about learning new parenting skills, and now I was obsessed with learning them. I was on a mission to find skills I could apply to make a difference in my children's desire to cooperate.

Do you know how many parenting books there are? There is no end to them.

I asked myself, "If all the parenting books teach the same thing, then why are there so many? If they teach something different, then which is the best?"

I read book after book, garnering what advice I considered useful out of each and testing it on my children. Then I noticed my children started to do crazy things, like, ask for my advice and talk and spend time with me. I actually started to enjoy being around them and even looked forward to spending time with them.

Fortunately, my wife was on board with all this transitioning I was trying to bring about. We discovered that parenting will always be challenging, but it doesn't have to be frustrating. We found that parenting did not have to be drudgery. Craziest thing: we started to enjoy it.

Fast forward a few years – ok, a lot of years. My children are grown now, with families of their own. Just for the record, they turned out pretty good; responsible, patient; good parents themselves. They serve in their communities and try to make a difference in other people's lives. No addictions or jail time that I'm aware of. They are my best friends and I still love spending time with them. I feel blessed that I recognized the need to make changes when I did.

One day I realized I had accumulated a great deal of valuable knowledge that I had been keeping to myself. So I decided to share it with the world by writing a book. I know, another parenting book, right? *But this one was different. Honest!* I took the best parts out of the best books I had read, and made them easy to understand with step-by-step instructions. My audience was parents who were in the same situation I was once in: somewhere between "*What do I do now?*" and "*I'm at the end of my rope,*" but did not have time to study and research.

The book: *How to Get Kids to Behave – The Manual that was Supposed to Come with Kids* was born.

Soon afterwards, I landed a job working for Utah State University teaching parenting workshops.

The book you are reading has been expanded and organized differently than my first book. This book contains some of the same material as my first book (some things you just can't improve on) along with a lot of additional information including *The 3-Step Formula*. Let me give you a sense of what you are about to learn.

Four Emotional Needs

All children have four emotional needs that must be met. If you meet these needs in positive ways, your children will stop misbehaving and start cooperating. Here are the four emotional needs:

1. A sense of belonging
2. A sense of personal power
3. To be heard and understood
4. Limits and boundaries

These needs are hard-wired into every child. You know how your child whines, teases, interrupts, ignores, talks back and treats others with disrespect? These negative behaviors are not random. They all have a purpose.

They are your child's way of saying, "Mom. Dad. I need you to meet my needs." Misbehavior is not the actual problem. It is a symptom of a deeper issue. *Children misbehave because their emotional needs are not being properly met.*

The 3-Step Parenting Formula

I have developed a formula to help you meet your children's emotional needs and improve behavior. I call it *The 3-Step Parenting Formula*. Here are the three steps:

1. Build a strong relationship with your children
2. Teach them life skills, good values, and desirable behavior
3. Skillfully correct them when their behavior is displeasing

Now watch how these steps are tied together. The key to effective correcting is effective teaching. The key to effective teaching is to have a strong relationship with your children.

If correcting unwanted behavior isn't working well, take a close look at your teaching. Teaching is the foundation of correcting. It's tough to correct a child's behavior if he doesn't understand exactly what is expected.

If your teaching seems to fall on deaf ears, focus on your relationship. It's hard to get kids to listen when your relationship is broken. They may look like they're listening, but they really won't care what you're saying. Relationship is the foundation of teaching and correcting. If your relationship is weak, teaching and correcting will be futile.

The mistake parents often make is focusing their attention on correcting their children's unwanted behavior when the relationship they have with their children is on shaky ground. Children often ignore, argue, talk back, or act defiantly when corrected by someone with whom they have a weak relationship. For that reason, parents need to focus on strengthening weak relationships before putting more effort into correcting bad behavior.

As you put The 3-Step Parenting Formula into practice, you can expect to see unwanted behavior decline and cooperation improve. No longer will you wonder what to do. Your self-doubts will fade and your confidence will grow. You will bring the fun back into parenting.

There is Much More at Stake

Up to now I've suggested that if you follow The 3-Step Parenting Formula, misbehavior will decrease and cooperation will increase, making parenting more enjoyable. But the power of The 3-Step Parenting Formula goes beyond that. It will help you to give your children the knowledge to recognize life's dangers and the ability to avoid them.

There are forces at work to entice children to do things that promise a thrill or provide immediate pleasure, but have long-lasting, harmful and addictive results. Peer pressure is causing many children and teens to make bad choices. The need for capable, effective parents has never been greater.

More than likely, your children will be offered opioids like OxyContin, Percocet, fentanyl or heroin. Other harmful and addictive drugs will become easily available to them like marijuana, ecstasy, cocaine, bath salts, methamphetamine, and more. Chances are good that someone will try to talk your children into trying alcohol, smoking, vaping, sexting, having sex, joining a gang, or committing a crime. Your kids will find out how easy it is to access pornography, how quickly they can lose weight by purging, and how they can reduce anxiety by cutting. Cyber bullying has become an issue with which all children on social media are familiar. And tragically, there is an epidemic of children contemplating suicide to escape emotional pain. You can't be there to protect them all the time.

Many parents do not know, do not believe, or will not admit that their children are exposed to so much harm. And even if they are aware, many do not know what to do. The 3-Step Parenting Formula will show you the skills and provide the knowledge you need to give your kids the best chance of living a life free from these kinds of problems. I hope you're starting to realize how important it is for you to be an intentional, positive force in your children's lives.

In 1990, Barbara Bush, wife of President George H. W. Bush, addressed the graduates of Wellesley College. In her address she said, "But whatever the era, whatever the times, one thing will never change: Fathers and mothers, if you have children, they must come first. You must read to your children and you must hug your children and you must love your children. Your success as a family, our success as a society, depends not on what happens in the White House but on what happens inside your house.[1]"

I am writing this book to help you strengthen your family. A strong family is built on strong relationships between every member of the family. When there are strong relationships within the family, everyone cares for each other, they step up to help each other, they encourage each other, listen to worries, applaud efforts, celebrate successes, and comfort each other in times of sorrow. Your home will be a place of refuge, understanding, learning and love. It will be a place where children can make mistakes without fear of criticism; where they can overcome challenges and grow into capable adults. It will be a place where you and your children cry together, laugh together, experience joy together, and face seemingly insurmountable trials together.

All children will come face to face with some form of seduction promising instant gratification that will undoubtedly result in long-term unhappiness. Children who come from strong families will recognize those situations and will be prepared and know what to do to avoid the traps. They will have adopted values to guide their lives and will have learned how to defend those values. They will have greater self-control and more power to resist temptation – even in the face of peer pressure. They will understand the consequences of giving into temptation because they will have been taught by parents with whom they have strong relationships. Children from strong families will have no need to numb emotional pain with drugs, alcohol, or pornography.

Parents who are at the head of strong families have few regrets and are much less likely to say at some point down the road, "If only I had…" or to wonder, ""What if I had done it differently."

This book will help you instill in your children the desire to do the right thing even when you're not around, and that will give you peace of mind.

Less frustration, more peace of mind – that's what you can expect from reading this book.

The next chapter begins your life-changing adventure. I'm very excited for you because I know what's ahead. Let's get started.

2

The Four Emotional Needs

This chapter answers the question: Why do my children misbehave? Once you have that down, it's easier to understand how to get them to cooperate.

Before you can fix a problem, it's helpful to understand why the problem is happening. If your car is not running well, you've got to figure out *why* it's not running well before you can make the proper repair. If your child is not behaving well, it helps to know *why* he's not behaving well before attempting to do anything to improve his behavior. I want to teach you something I learned that caused me to see children in a whole new light. What I learned was so enlightening, that I cannot imagine anyone trying to change a child's behavior without first learning why kids misbehave in the first place. It all begins with four built-in needs of every child.

The Four Built-In Needs of Every Child

All children are born with four emotional needs that must be met. These needs are wired into every child's brain although they are not consciously aware of it. Every child craves to have these needs met. They can't help but seek after them. It's what they were born to do. It is one thing you can always count on. Knowing this can be very helpful because if you meet these needs in positive ways, cooperation will replace misbehavior. Here are the four needs:

A sense of belonging
A sense of personal power
To be heard and understood
Limits and boundaries

Let's take a close look at each one.

A Sense of Belonging

Every child has a need to feel a sense of belonging. To a child, belonging means to feel important, noticed, included, accepted and loved. Every child craves to feel needed, valued, and recognized as a part of the family. Each one yearns for his parent's undivided attention and approval. When a child does not feel a sense of belonging, he feels ignored, left out, forgotten and rejected, and a child cannot bear to feel that way. So even though a child is not consciously aware of it, he is constantly looking for ways to feel like he belongs.

If a child does not feel a sense of belonging, he will go after it on his own. Every waking hour will be spent exploring methods (or behaviors) that will lead to a sense of belonging. When he discovers a behavior that results in a sense of belonging, he will repeat that behavior again and again. For example, he has learned from the day he was born that crying will cause you to give him your exclusive attention. As he gets older and crying no longer works as well, he intensifies the crying making it louder and longer, hoping to regain the attention he craves. He will add whining, teasing, and acting helpless as his *method of operation* to receive your attention, and continue to use it while it works.

A Sense of Personal Power

Every child has a need to feel a sense of personal power. Where a sense of belonging means to feel included, a sense of personal power means to feel significant, in charge of one's self, having the freedom to choose; to feel empowered. Children have a keen sense of observation. They observe that grownups have all the power – the power to command what to eat, when to eat, when to go to bed, when to get up, what to wear, what to do, what not to do. Children decide early in their lives that they want to feel power too. It happens to all children. It's a basic need. It's how they start to become independent, and after all, ultimately, isn't that what we want them to become: independent, able to think for themselves, take care of themselves, and make decisions? That starts with personal power. The need for personal power is wired into every child.

If a child does not feel a sense of personal power, she will go after it, and the easiest way to feel personal power is to simply say "no" to a request or command. When she discovers that refusing to obey brings a feeling of personal power, she will repeat that behavior. Choosing to obey is the one thing she has complete control over no matter what her age.

How Children Meet their Own Needs

Children start out life knowing nothing. They learn through observing and exploring. They are like little scientists, always experimenting. From their failures they draw the conclusion: "Hmmm. This didn't meet my needs. Make a mental note to avoid doing it in the future." From their successes they draw the conclusion: "Ah-ha! This is how I can belong. This is how I can feel personal power. If it worked once, it should work again." Their successful experiments and repeated actions are what we call behavior.

Children have undeveloped minds. That's a good thing because you can have a big influence on how those minds are developed. However, that can be a bad thing when left on their own, because children make mistaken conclusions from their experiments. Children who are compelled to meet their own needs for belonging and personal power usually do so in ways that parents disapprove.

For example, a child might conclude that hitting, teasing, throwing tantrums, whining and getting into mischief is a good way to get mom or dad's attention, and getting their attention gives him a sense of belonging. Children learn that although these behaviors bring an angry reaction from parents, it is better than no attention. Angry attention is better than no attention.

A child might conclude that arguing, ignoring, being defiant, and doing the opposite of whatever he is directed to do builds his sense of personal power. Imagine what power a child must feel knowing he can make Mom and Dad angry anytime he wants. He learns how to push their buttons. He takes pleasure in teasing his sibling in order to get a predictable angry or negative reaction from his parents. I call that getting a "power fix".

Now that you know about these two basic needs (the need to feel a sense of belonging and the need to feel a sense of personal power) you can do things to meet these needs in positive ways. Children don't care HOW these needs are met, only that they ARE met. Granted, they will still explore, experiment, create, make mistakes, get into trouble, and have as much fun as they can. That's how kids learn and grow. But once these two basic needs are met, there's really no reason for children to try to meet these needs on their own by repeatedly misbehaving.

Children misbehave when they are left on their own to figure out how to meet these two built-in needs. Children behave "good" when their parents, caregivers, babysitters and teachers do the proper things to meet their needs in positive ways.

Misbehavior is not random. Your child is on a mission to feel a sense of belonging and personal power. All the arguing, interrupting, whining, talking back, ignoring, defying and other misbehaviors are symptoms of unmet needs. If you focus only on the bad behavior by yelling, spanking, reminding, nagging and punishing, the bad behavior might go away for a while, but it will return. Why? Because the child must still meet her needs, and if misbehaving is the only way those needs are going to be met, then misbehavior is **guaranteed** to happen again and again.

However, if you focus on the deeper issue, helping your children meet their two basic needs, the bad behavior will go away and stay away. Furthermore, when children don't have to concern themselves with meeting their own needs, they can focus more of their attention on exploring, experimenting and learning – the things that foster self-confidence and independence.

I hope you've been asking yourself, *"So, how do I meet these two needs?"*

The answer is by strengthening the relationships you have with your children. Section 1 is dedicated to explaining how to strengthen relationships with children.

To be heard and understood

All children have a need to be heard and understood. They cannot meet this need on their own. It requires another person. When children are in distress and their need to be heard and understood is not met, they can become frustrated and angry. If this need continues to go unmet for a long time, the stored up pain can result in defiance, depression, hostility and addictions. However, by meeting a child's need to be heard and understood, the child is given the freedom to let go of his distressing feelings, and his ability to solve his own problem increases greatly.

The way a parent can meet this need is by practicing listening skills. Listening provides healing. Listening is life-changing. Listening is one of the most important skills a parent can learn. When a child comes to you in distress, he doesn't want you to agree or disagree; he doesn't need your opinion or advice. He doesn't want you to "fix it". What he needs is for you to listen and show that you understand. Chapter 6 – Acknowledge Negative Feelings, explains in detail how to meet this need.

Limits and Boundaries

All children have a need for limits and boundaries. Clear, enforced limits and boundaries make children feel safe, secure, and confident that their parents care about them. Limits and boundaries are necessary to provide a sense of order in the household, keep kids safe, and teach respect for each other. As the parent, you set limits and boundaries by teaching children about them, why they exist, and correcting children when they test those limits and boundaries. In other words, you set and enforce desired expectations (or rules). Expectations actually teach kids to set limits for themselves, which is otherwise known as self-discipline. Expectations teach self-discipline.

One thing that is handy to know is this: children don't recognize limits and boundaries until they test them. That's why it's important for you to understand how to set and enforce expectations in loving and effective ways. Section 2 explains how to teach desirable behavior by setting expectations and making rules, and Section 3 focuses on skillfully correcting children when they don't follow expectations or obey the rules.

When your children's emotional needs are not being met in positive ways, they will make it known through their behavior; or rather, their misbehavior.

When a child whines for your attention, she is saying, "I need to feel a sense of belonging."

When a child ignores your request to get ready for bed, she is saying, "I'll do what I want because it's how I get my power fix."

When a child smacks his sibling, it may be out of frustration from not feeling heard and understood.

When a child makes a sandbox on the kitchen floor from a bag of flour, she is saying, "What rule?"

If you want to replace misbehavior with cooperation you must meet these four needs. If fact, the *only* thing you need to do to turn behavior around is to meet these four needs. Anything else is extra, needless work. You can cut out everything that does not serve to meet these needs. That means you will never have to scream, spank, punish, lecture, criticize, bribe, or threaten because they do not serve to meet any of the four needs.

Now that you know the "Why" behind your child's misbehaver, you can address the "How". That's where The 3-Step Parenting Formula comes in, and that's when the fun begins.

3

The 3-Step Parenting Formula

The 3-Step Parenting Formula is designed to show you how to meet the four emotional needs that are built in to every child. When you meet these needs in positive ways, your child's misbehavior will decrease and her desire to cooperate will increase. I developed The 3-Step Parenting Formula to help you understand and remember three important steps. The remainder of this book is organized around them. Here are the three steps:

1. Build a strong relationship with your children
2. Teach them life skills, good values, and desirable behavior
3. Skillfully correct them when their behavior is displeasing

There you have it. That's how to get kids to behave. That's how to get kids to cooperate. That's how to raise good kids. Confused? Let me explain further by showing you the following illustration[1]:

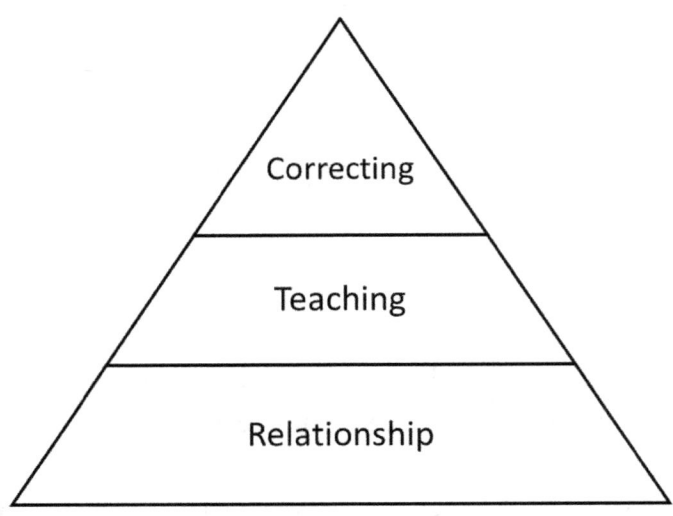

The three levels of this pyramid correspond to the three steps in The 3-Step Parenting Formula. Notice the order.

Correcting

"Correcting" is at the top, meaning, skillfully correcting your children when their behavior is displeasing. Correcting serves to meet your children's emotional need for limits and boundaries. Children have a tendency to test the limits and boundaries you set for them. Correcting helps them understand they are expected to stay within those limits and boundaries.

Correcting is how you *enforce* rules and expectations.

You'll notice that "Correcting" is at the top of the pyramid, and therefore, the smallest part of the pyramid. That is to illustrate that compared to the other two levels, correcting should receive the least amount of focus; the least amount of attention. That's right. More effort should be given to teaching, and the majority of your attention should be given to strengthening relationships.

An important thing to remember about correcting is this: *Effective correcting depends on effective teaching.* There must be effective teaching before correcting will work. If you are finding that your children don't respond well when you try to correct their misbehavior, rather than intensifying your effort to get them to mind, focus on the level below correcting: Teaching.

Teaching is the foundation of correcting. When correcting is built on teaching, two things will happen: 1) children will understand what is expected of them, and 2) they will respond more positively to correcting. Section 3 is all about Skillfully Correcting. But before you can correct behavior, you must teach the kind of behavior you expect.

Teaching

"Teaching" is the middle tier. There are three areas of teaching: 1) teaching life skills, 2) teaching good values, and 3) teaching desirable behavior. Teaching desirable behavior is how you *set* rules and expectations.

An important thing to remember about teaching is this: *Effective teaching depends on a strong relationship with your child.* There must be a strong relationship before teaching can be effective. If you are finding that your teaching is falling on deaf ears, or that your child doesn't seem to care about what you teach, rather than spending more time and effort trying to get your child to listen and learn, focus on the level below teaching: "Relationship."

"Relationship" is the foundation of "Teaching." It is the biggest level of the pyramid to remind us that strengthening relationships should be given the most attention. If your child doesn't have a strong connection with you, she is unlikely to be receptive to the expectations you want her to learn. When teaching is built on a strong relationship, you will enjoy teaching and your child will care about and remember what you teach. Section 2 is all about teaching, but before you can teach effectively, you must work on strengthening your relationship with your child.

A student in one of my workshops asked, "My kids don't listen to me. I tell them to do something and they just ignore me. What can I do?"

I addressed the class and said, "That's such a common problem among parents these days, isn't it? I see it all the time, don't you?"

Then pointing to the pyramid I said, "When we try to correct our children's behavior and it's just not working, should we intensify our correcting? No. What should we do? We should focus our attention on the level below Correcting, which is Teaching. Do our children really understand the behavior we expect from them? What if our children pay no attention to the rules we set or to the behavior we expect? Do we teach harder? Longer? Louder? No. What should we do? We should focus our attention on the level below Teaching, which is Relationship. Are we intentionally working on strengthening the relationship we have with our children? The foundation to effective correcting and teaching is Relationship. Without a strong relationship, teaching falls on deaf ears and correcting misbehavior is exhausting and ineffective. But when there's a strong relationship between children and parents, children develop a desire to please their parents and feel bad when they let their parent's down. In other words, children want to cooperate. But that's not all. When we have a good relationship, we enjoy being around our kids. We laugh together. When they get home they tell us about their day. They confide in us. We experience the deep satisfaction we always hoped raising children would bring us."

Relationship

"Relationship" is on the ground floor of the pyramid, suggesting that "Strengthening Relationships" is the foundation for teaching and correcting. Shout it from the mountain tops. Write it in your journal. Tell everyone you know. Send it into the abyss of social media: *Strengthening relationships is the foundation for teaching and correcting.* The effectiveness of teaching and correcting depends on the strength of your relationships with your children. When you have a strong relationship with your children, they develop a desire to please you. They won't want to disappoint you. They will be open to what you teach, and responsive to being corrected. I have devoted Section 1 to strengthening relationships.

In Section 1, I introduce five things you can do that will dramatically improve the relationships you have with your children. I refer to them as "**principles**." A principle is a guiding requirement to make something happen.

Here are five guiding requirements, or principles, that are going to strengthen your relationships. I call them, "The Incredibly Powerful and Effective Five Principles for Strengthening Relationships and Making Teaching and Correcting much more Effective." We can just call them *The 5 Principles* for short. Here they are:

1. **Spend one-on-one time with each child.** This is quality, one-on-one time on a regular basis.

2. **Spend family time together.** Do activities as a family, including dinner together and weekly family meetings.

3. **Acknowledge Negative Feelings.** Learn how to listen and respond to your children to help them "let go" of their anger and negative feelings.

4. Get to know your kids. Get to know your kids' likes, dislikes, fears, opinions and worries.

5. Make positive deposits. By doing things that build trust in your relationship, you make deposits. By doing things that decrease the level of trust in your relationship, you make withdrawals.

The 5 Principles can be applied to children of all ages, from toddlers to teens. Some specific parts of these principles are age-specific and better applied to children than to teens. I've tried to make those parts obvious. I think you'll find that no matter how mild or obnoxious your children's misbehaviors are, you will be amazed at the results that will come from applying, "The 5 Principles." Each principle will serve to make your relationships with your children stronger, and a stronger relationship means a stronger, happier family.

"The 5 Principles" will help you meet three of your children's emotional needs mentioned in the previous chapter:

1. The need to feel a sense of belonging
2. The need to feel a sense of personal power
3. The need to feel heard and understood

Section 1 deals with Relationships. Section 2 talks about Teaching, and Section 3 focuses on Correcting.

Section 1

Build a Strong Relationship with your Children

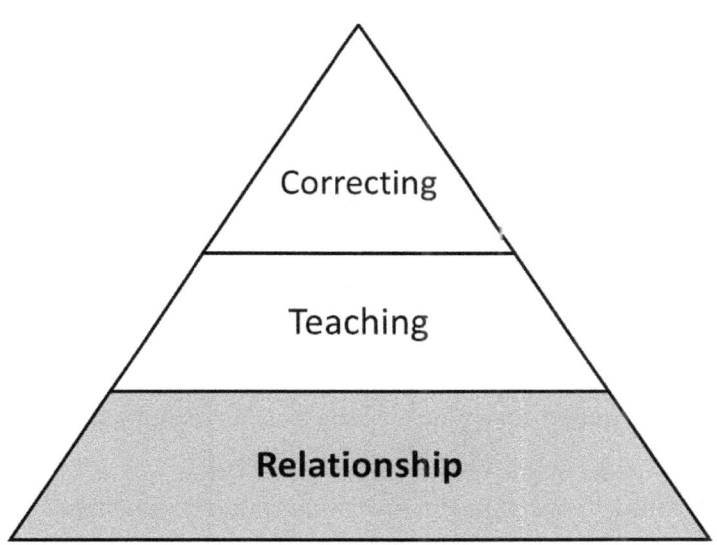

Everything depends on relationships. Strong relationships are the best way to keep misbehavior from happening. They are the foundation to effective teaching and skillful correcting. When children have a strong connection with you, they are open to your guidance and react favorably when you correct their behavior. Children gain a healthy respect for you and a desire to please you. *No amount of teaching-skills or correcting-skills can make up for a weak relationship.*

When your children feel connected to you, they will develop higher self-esteem, get along better with siblings, do better in school, and handle stress better. They will also be better prepared to withstand all the negative influences they will face when they are not under your watchful eye. The best protection for children against negative influences is a strong relationship with you.

The 5 Principles will help you strengthen the relationships you have with your children, and when you strengthen relationships, you meet your children's four emotional needs in positive ways.

There is a common element to all 5 principles: *They all require your time.* There is no getting around it. There is no shortcut. In order to strengthen the relationships you have with your children, you're going to have to invest your time. Let me put it another way, if you do not make time to strengthen relationships, you will spend at least the same amount of time dealing with unwanted behaviors.

4

Principle 1: Spend One-On-One Time with Each Child

Spending personal time with each child communicates that you value them and consider them to be an important part of the family. Using this principle is the number one, irreplaceable, best way to meet each child's need to feel a sense of belonging. It gives them what they most desperately want from you: your complete attention. If they can get that, their negative attention-seeking behaviors are no longer needed.

Spending personal time with each child also helps to meet their need to feel a sense of personal power. Personal power is the freedom to choose. When you allow the child to choose the activity, you reduce the child's desire to meet that need in negative ways.

What I mentioned earlier bears repeating: If you don't spend one-on-one time with each child, you will end up spending at least that same amount of time dealing with their negative behaviors. Wouldn't you rather spend time preventing problems than fixing them? Wouldn't you rather enjoy having a good time with your children rather than fighting with them?

If you are having issues with your child such as whining, clinging, teasing, not listening, back-talking, defiance, or fighting with siblings, spending personal time with your child is the first place to start, because these are not discipline problems, they are relationship problems.

You won't believe what a difference practicing this principle will make in your child's behavior. Here's the principle in a little more detail: *Each parent spends uninterrupted time with each child, every day, doing what the child likes to do.*

Here is the ideal way to use this principle:

1. Let your children know there is a new sheriff in town (you!) and things are going to be different around here. From now on, this new sheriff is going to spend one-on-one time with each child as many days in the week as possible. If there are two parents, then each child can expect time from both sheriffs.

2. Give the principle a more personal name, like, "Daddy-Kaitlyn Time" and "Mommy-Kaitlyn Time."

3. Choose a time every day and put it on the calendar so each child can look forward to it. That's right; you will schedule your day around each child's one-on-one time with you. I want to impress upon you the importance of this principle.

4. Spend uninterrupted time with each child every day for at least 15 minutes. You may feel like the bad guy when you have to tell your child that your time together is over. Here's an idea to help you with that. Set a timer. Then when the timer goes off, the timer is the bad guy, not you. Even better, have your child set the timer.

5. Give 100% of your attention to your child. No distractions. No siblings. No cell phones.

6. Let your child decide how your time is to be spent. If she can't think of anything, then you get to offer a couple of choices: "Hmmm. Do you want to play some catch or throw the Frisbee?" This might be a good time to teach life skills: "We could bake up some brownies or how about we make some cookies?"

7. This is not a time to talk about their dirty room, chores not completed, or needed self-improvements – unless they bring it up.

8. Never threaten to cancel personal time as a way to improve behavior: "If you misbehave like that again, no Daddy-Kaitlyn Time today." That is like saying, "If you continue to stay sick, I will stop giving you medicine."

Finding Time

Okay, let's get real. Finding time can be difficult.

As hard as it is with the pressures of earning a living, household responsibilities and a busy schedule, if you want to strengthen your relationships with your children, you have to free up the time, every day, to spend one-on-one time with each child. If you make strengthening your relationships a top priority, you'll find the time. If you must postpone house cleaning, forgo Facebook time, cancel your cable, reschedule your workout, or even earn less money (I know, it was difficult for me to even suggest that) to find the time to spend with each child, the rewards will be worth it. If yours is a 2-parent family, both of you should spend time with each child daily. For some of you, this might be asking a lot, maybe even too much. But I would not be so bold in making this appeal if I wasn't so sure that the sacrifice would be worth it.

With that said, if it is impossible to spend time with each of your children every day, do it as often as you can. Just remember, the more often and regularly you can spend one-on-one time with each child, the better they will respond.

Distractions

Sometimes distractions cannot be avoided. However, keep in mind that one reason this principle works so well is because you are satisfying your child's need for your total attention. Your child should not have to compete with anyone or anything. If you are mentally preparing a grocery list or talking on the phone and only half-focused on your child, your child will feel your divided interest. If that happens, this principle will lose its effectiveness and you'll be wasting your time.

If you have other children, consider putting on a fun DVD to keep them busy, or getting someone to look after them. The other children, however, will be better behaved knowing they just had, or will soon have, their turn with you.

Activities

Let your child decide how you are to spend your time together. You will be entering her world and doing what she likes to do, so be ready to play. Depending on her age, you might build a tower with blocks, read a book together, kick around the soccer ball, or just talk. Your time together should be face to face. No TV. Be prepared to give your child a choice between two activities if she can't think of one. "Would you like to play a game or read a book?"

Here is a list of some of the things that my wife and I have done with our children. You'll notice that some of them require more time than 15 minutes. We have never regretted any extra time we spent with our children.

1. Lie next to each child in their bed at night and just talk
2. Lie on the trampoline or grass at night with blankets and pillows and look at the stars
3. Play catch
4. Play a game – backgammon was a favorite of some of my children. We would also play the "matching" game with Old Maid cards – turn them all face down and take turns flipping over two cards, trying to find a matching pair
5. Throw the Frisbee
6. Shoot some hoops
7. Read together
8. Take a trip to the library. Check out a book on "activities for children" and read it together. Choose an activity and do it. Find some good story books to check out as well
9. Bake something – cake, cookies, brownies
10. Build something with blocks or Lego's
11. Draw or color something
12. Go to a golf course. Practice putting on the putting green, hit a bucket of balls, or play a round
13. Build a snowman
14. Make snow angels
15. Have a picnic – outdoors or indoors
16. Visit a museum
17. Take the dog to a dog training class together

18. Take a walk, or walk the dog together
19. Write a letter together to someone you both know, like Grandma, or a friend
20. Look at family photos together
21. Sing songs
22. Tell stories about when your child was a toddler or a baby
23. Simply hold your child
24. Build a blanket fort
25. Plant flower or vegetable seeds. Tend it together – or plant a garden
26. Go to the park
27. Finger Paint
28. Take pictures or video – make a movie
29. Visit an aquarium
30. Put together a puzzle
31. Build a fire together – then make s'mores
32. Build something with wood – maybe a bird house
33. Make homemade pizza
34. Rake leaves and jump in the pile
35. Make water balloons. Play catch with one as you slowly back farther away from each other.
36. Go on a bike ride
37. Find a fruit tree and pick fruit together – apples, apricots, pears, etc.
38. Have fun with Play Dough
39. Spa time: Paint fingernails and toenails. Do hair and makeup. Be outrageous.
40. Go on a hike
41. Attend a baseball, basketball, soccer, or football game
42. Go fishing
43. Go out for ice cream sundaes or ice cream cones

44. Go out for pie, bagels, donuts, pizza or burgers
45. Look at things under a magnifying glass
46. Go horseback riding
47. Blow bubbles
48. Paint a picture by numbers together
49. Go to a theater or dance performance
50. Wash the car
51. Do dishes together
52. Clean out a closet together
53. Fly a kite
54. Jump rope
55. Exercise together
56. Color with crayons or colored pencils
57. Go bowling – or set up a bowling alley in your hall with empty 2-liter plastic bottles and a softball.
58. Play Simon Says
59. Play "I Spy"
60. Listen to music and play homemade instruments together
61. Start a journal with each child
62. Prepare a family meal together
63. Start a collection
64. Play with sidewalk chalk
65. Play tetherball
66. Play ping pong
67. Indoor golf (putters only)
68. Tell jokes
69. Play hillbilly golf (Google it)
70. Go jogging together – enter a 1 mile or 5K race
71. Attend an auction together and bid on something
72. Visit a play ground
73. Go to a movie

74. Feed the ducks at a local pond
75. Have them teach you something they know but you don't
76. Write a blog
77. Write a song
78. Write a story
79. Write a poem
80. Experiment with a new recipe – get outrageous
81. Go swimming together
82. Go camping in the backyard or in the woods
83. Bathe the dog

Here are some situations to avoid because they will cause bad feelings and lead to bad behavior:

1. Spending personal time with one child but not with another.
2. Spending noticeably more time with one child than with another.
3. Cancelling personal time when the child is looking forward to it.

I was teaching a parenting workshop and one of the participants told this story after he had learned about spending one-on-one time with each child. He was a divorced father who had visiting rights to see his three children for three hours on weekends. He said this past weekend he did something different. He told his children that he was going to spend one half hour with each one individually, doing what they wanted to do. Then he would spend the remainder of the time doing something with them all together. He said it was the most enjoyable time he had ever spent with his children.

Another parent told me that he started spending one-on-one time with his "difficult" 10 year old son. Then some "crazy" things started happening, like, his son started asking for his advice, and they started having conversations that didn't end in arguments. He said his relationship is improving and he is starting to actually enjoy being around his son.

This is a powerful principle and if you practice it, you will experience amazing results.

5

Principle 2: Spend Family Time Together

Principle #2 is the same as Principle #1 but done with the whole family instead of with each child individually. But make no mistake, it does not replace Principle #1.

You may feel that doing something with your entire family is inviting fighting, complaining, stress, and not worth the effort. However, if you have been practicing Principle #1 and have been giving your children the positive attention they crave, there will be less fighting and complaining during family time because your children will no longer have a need to compete for your attention. That means less stress for you and more fun for everyone.

Family Activities

Family activities promote family bonding and strengthen relationships between you and your children. They also strengthen relationships between your children and their siblings. Furthermore, they create good memories. Years later when your children are older, they will talk about the good times you spent doing things together. So remember to take pictures and record the events in a journal.

Family activities provide opportunities for having fun together, working together and solving problems together. They provide opportunities for children to help each other, encourage each other, listen to each other, solve problems, applaud efforts, and celebrate successes. Children can try new things without fear of criticism. Family activities are a necessary part of a strong family. Here are a few things we did in our family:

1. Pumpkin carving. Every Halloween, it was a tradition to carve pumpkins. One year I said, "You know what's fun about carving pumpkins? Throwing pumpkin guts!" Then I tossed some at the children, which started everyone throwing pumpkin guts. We made a tremendous mess, but man, was it fun. Then we had a family activity cleaning up our mess and cleaning off our clothes and hair – not as much fun.

2. Dancing. We cranked up the music and danced. It was a good way to show some creative expression and burn off some energy.

3. Blanket swinging. When the kids were small, my wife and I had each child lay on a blanket on the floor. Then Mother would grab the two corners of the blanket on her side (at the child's head) and I would grab the two corners on my side and we would swing our child back and forth in the blanket. After multiple turns by all the children, Mother and I were pretty worn out, but the kids sure loved it.

4. Singing. We tried harmony and sang choruses of "Row, Row, Row, Your Boat."

Other activities you might consider:

5. Movie night with lots of popcorn.

6. Bowling
7. Swimming and water amusement parks
8. Picnics
9. Hiking
10. Biking
11. Spending time at the park
12. Going to amusement parks
13. Going out for ice cream
14. Flag football
15. Kickball
16. Kite flying
17. Miniature golf
18. Badminton
19. Around the world Frisbee. Make a huge circle and toss two Frisbees around the circle at the same time.
20. Jump rope.
21. Red Rover
22. Duck-duck-goose
23. Ice blocking – get a block of ice. Put a towel over the top and slide down a grassy hill.
24. Inner tubing down snowy hills
25. Hide-and-go-seek
26. Hopscotch
27. Huckle-buckle beanstalk
28. Musical chairs
29. Bean bag toss
30. Go to the zoo

31. Go camping
32. Go to the library
33. Go to the children's museum
34. Attend parades
35. Watch fireworks
36. Go to the rodeo
37. Fishing
38. Build one big snowman or multiple little ones
39. Indoor golf – putting only
40. Christmas caroling
41. Attend a baseball game – no baseball game is complete without a hot dog or nachos.
42. Easter egg hunt

Eat Dinner Together

Eating dinner together as a family provides opportunities for talking, catching up, and reconnecting. Family meal-time helps children feel loved, safe and secure. Studies have shown when families regularly eat together and the conversation is positive, children are more likely to exhibit good behavior.

Here are some guidelines to get the most out of family dinners:

If you don't usually eat together, start by scheduling one meal per week and increase the number as you are able. Eating together can happen at breakfast, lunch or dinner. Choose the meal that gives you the most time to talk and connect. Once you decide which meal you are going to eat together, mark it on your calendar like you would any other event. If you plan for it, it is more likely to happen.

Involve the children in dinner preparation. It can be a great teaching opportunity. Teach your children how to plan, shop for and prepare meals, and then let them try it on their own. Be patient when they make mistakes. Don't criticize. Teach about food safety: to wash hands before preparing food and how some foods need to be stored in the refrigerator or freezer. Teach about kitchen safety like how to properly use a knife. Teach how to properly use kitchen appliances.

Do not use dinner time to correct misbehavior that may have happened earlier in the day. Focus on enjoying each other's company.

Invite friends and other extended family to join you on occasion. My children will tell you a story about the time we invited a family in our neighborhood over for dinner. We put a clean, plastic tablecloth on the table and asked everyone to wash their hands well. There were no plates or utensils on the table. Spaghetti, garlic bread and a tossed salad were put in the middle of the table with serving spoons. Everyone was invited to take some spaghetti, spaghetti sauce, salad and garlic bread and put it on the table in front of them. Forks were outlawed. Everyone had to eat with their fingers. In a culture where eating with your fingers is frowned upon, we had great fun breaking the rule – the kids especially. Our Mom and Dad guests looked a little uncertain but by the end of the meal they looked like they kind of got the hang of it.

You can have pizza night, Chinese food night, sandwich night or mac and cheese night. Order out occasionally, but learn to make food from scratch. Don't be afraid to experiment. Learn to make new meals from healthy recipes.

Turn off distractions like the TV, computer, tablets and cell phones during mealtimes. Keep toys, electronic devices and books off the table.

Pleasant conversation at family meal time can be a good way to learn about what your kids are doing and thinking.

A good way to get family members talking is to ask a question for everyone to answer: "So, tell us one good thing that happened to you today."

Questions get people thinking. As a result, interesting conversations can occur. Go around the table and give everyone a chance to respond. Remember, no criticizing, lecturing, or arguing. Just listen and try to understand.

Here is a list of possible subjects to get you started:

"What is one good thing and one bad thing that happened to you today?"

"If you could do anything you wanted, what would that be?"

"What was the hardest thing you did today?"

"Tell us something that made you laugh today."

"If you could be any animal, what would you be?"

"If you could visit any place, where would that be?"

"What food do you love, and what food do you hate?"

"If you could have any three wishes, what would they be?"

"If you won a million dollars, what would you do with it?"

"What is the one chore that you hate the most?"

"If someone asked you to suggest a name for their new baby, what would it be?" (Not that anyone is making an announcement.)

"What is one kind deed that you did today?"

Consider doing this: Ask your family to add some questions to this list, print the list, cut out each question and put in a jar. At the beginning of dinner have someone draw a question out of the jar.

Then go around the table and have each person answer the question.

Here's another activity you can try around the dinner table. It's called "Hot Seat." It's like truth or dare without the dare. One person is chosen to be in the hot seat. Then everyone else takes turns asking that person one question. The person in the hot seat must answer that question. When everyone has had a turn to ask a question, the hot seat rotates to the next person and everyone else gets a chance to ask one question to that person. Everyone around the table gets a chance to be in the hot seat – even Mom and Dad.

Have Weekly Family Meetings

A strong family is built on strong relationships within the family. Weekly family meetings help build strong relationships. They give everyone a voice in making decisions that affect the family, which helps meet children's needs for both a sense of personal power and a sense of belonging. They also provide a setting in which you can teach life skills, good values, and desirable behavior. No other event will bring your family closer together. And family meetings can be quite fun.

Here's how weekly family meetings work. Once every week, gather everyone in the family together. Ideally, this should happen on the same day at the same time so everyone can plan and schedule around it. Sunday evenings work well for some families, while others find it best to do it on a week night.

Hold your family meeting wherever it is convenient and comfortable, with limited distractions. You may want to move the location from time to time for a little variety. The living room, kitchen, or backyard make good spots.

Some families find that holding weekly family meetings during dinner produce too many distractions: "Please pass the meatloaf."

Family meetings don't need to take a long time. Depending on your agenda, one meeting could be as short as 15 minutes or take up the entire evening.

The Basics

A family meeting is a way for all family members to reconnect, give and receive compliments, update calendars, learn new things, solve problems, and have fun. Following are activities that will contribute to the success of your Family Meetings:

Appreciation Time

Everyone takes a moment at the beginning of each family meeting and shares one thing they appreciated about each family member during the past week. The first time you do this, it might seem a little awkward for family members who are not used to giving or receiving compliments. However, as you continue to do this every week, it won't be long before everyone will look forward to hearing something good about themselves – especially from their siblings.

Mom might get the ball rolling by saying something like this:

"I appreciate Dad for spending his lunch-hour last week to take Suzi to the dentist. That really helped me out. Aubrey, I noticed you made a real good effort to get all your homework done this past week. Keep up the good work. I appreciate Suzi for helping Allison find her shoes on that day we were in a hurry to get out of here. You helped both of us. And Allison, I appreciate you helping me fix dinner the other night. We had fun, didn't we?"

Then dad, Aubrey, Suzi and Allison will each take a turn and tell one thing they appreciate about each of the other family members. Expressing appreciation only takes a few minutes and is a good way to set a positive tone for the rest of the meeting.

Calendar Time

Family Meetings are a good time to coordinate everyone's schedule for the following week. Bring the family calendar to the meeting and write down everything that needs to be remembered: dance lessons, basketball practice, school play rehearsals, school projects due, doctor appointments, etc. Decide who is going to take whom and at what time. Make sure that your next family meeting is scheduled on your family calendar. During the week, keep the calendar where everyone can see it.

This is also good training for children to keep their own calendars to keep track of events in their own lives like babysitting, sleep-overs, birthday parties, and school assignments. They should bring their calendars to the family meeting.

This is the time to resolve scheduling conflicts rather than finding out later that you need to be in two places at the same time. Calendar Time will help avoid forgetting important events, help everyone get where they're supposed to be when they're supposed to be there, and eliminate chaos and anxiety.

Fun Time

When your children grow up and look back at past family meetings, the things they will remember most will not be calendar time, or even treat time. They will remember (and talk about) the fun times they shared together as a family. So make Fun Time a part of every family meeting. Fun Time will bond your family together. If you only have time to do one thing, do Fun Time. Fun Time can be as simple as going around the room and having everyone tell a joke, to something more ambitious like going for a bike ride. It should be the last item on your family meeting agenda. Try board games, card games like Uno, or a skill game like Jenga. For ideas, consider the following resources:

> Ask your kids for suggestions.
> Get ideas from another family who holds regular family meetings.
> Check out a book from the library about family activities.
> Do a Google search on, "Activities for kids" or "Family activities."

There are other things you can do to add value and variety to your family meetings. You can use family meetings for open discussion, to teach something, or to solve a problem. You can also invite a guest to attend or even invite a guest to give a presentation. After holding a few family meetings, you will find it beneficial to get the children involved by assigning family meeting roles (discussed below). The entire family meeting should be enjoyable. Your number one goal should be to make family meetings a time the whole family looks forward to.

Treat Time

Everyone enjoys treats, so be sure to make Treat Time part of every family meeting. Consider leaving Treat Time for the end of each family meeting or included during Fun Time. That way everyone will have something to look forward to. Treats can be anything delicious: cookies, cake, pie, ice cream, brownies, Rice

Krispy squares, or scones. (Or a new experimental recipe. Be adventurous). Ask family members for suggestions.

Add More Items to Your Agenda

After you feel comfortable with the basics, you can add more items to your agenda. In fact, start by adding an agenda. From this point forward, prepare an agenda for each family meeting. The agenda is to help you cover all the important activities and stay on track. You might want to put the agenda on the refrigerator for everyone to see and add items to talk about. Here is an example:

Agenda

Appreciation time
Calendar time
Open discussion
Teach value: Being kind
Fun and treat time

Open Discussion

Open Discussion is the opportunity for anyone to talk about anything. It can be used to ask for help in making a decision, register a complaint, present a problem and find a solution, make an announcement, or request help with something. Aunt Millie is coming to visit us for three days. How can we prepare? We are going to be painting the downstairs. What daily routines will need to be changed? There is not enough hot water to go around in the morning. What can we do so everyone gets a hot shower? We have a vacation coming up. What are some activities we would like to do? Every family member is encouraged to offer input.

Complaining and problem-solving can sometimes get volatile, so set some rules:

Let everyone know they are expected to use a calm voice.
Only one person gets to speak at a time.
Everyone will have a chance to offer their input.
Use "I Feel" statements – as discussed in the chapter 16.

When it comes to problem solving, give everyone a chance to offer a possible solution. The solution should not be a result of a majority vote. Majority vote means there are winners and losers, and you should avoid making anyone feel like a loser. Work together to find a solution that everyone can get behind (or at least live with) for at least one week. Once the decision is made, give it a week to see how it works, and then bring it up for discussion in the next family meeting.

If possible, let the children come up with the solution they are willing to try, even if you feel it is not the best solution. Sometimes the most effective training is to let children feel the consequences of their decisions and then make needed changes. Stress that what you decide as a family, you commit to as a family. This attitude will get everyone pulling together as a team. Solving problems together promotes family unity – even if the solution is not what you consider to be the best one. It is better to promote family unity than to have Mom and Dad dictate what they feel is the best and only solution. *Follow the guidelines to solving problems presented in Chapter 20.*

At the next family meeting, get everyone's opinion on how well the problem was solved. Do not say, "I told you so." Tweak the solution if needed and try it for another week. Once children get used to solving problems as a family, they will feel safe going to their siblings for opinions and advice. They will learn to solve problems among themselves.

Open Discussion is a great time to teach the skill of problem-solving. Group problem-solving involves various skills including listening, expressing one's point of view, understanding another person's point of view, creative thinking, coming up with possible solutions, analyzing possible consequences, compromising, and reaching consensus. Problem-solving is a skill that takes practice, and your family meetings will be a good training ground for that.

Teach Something

The weekly Family Meeting offers a good opportunity to teach. This is a good time for Mom or Dad to teach something that might be awkward or difficult under any other circumstance. This is where good values are learned and discussed. Consider announcing next week's topic and invite everyone to bring questions or comments they think of during the week.

Mom or Dad can offer a short lesson, but lessons do not need to be taught exclusively by them. After family meetings have become routine, each of the children should have an opportunity to teach something, depending on their age. Teaching is a good life-skill to have, and the family meeting is a good time to learn and practice. Additionally, the person who prepares and gives the lesson usually is the one who learns the most. You can assign someone a topic, or you can ask them to choose a topic in which they are interested. Give them plenty of time to prepare and offer help if needed. You may want to team-teach so the child doesn't feel so scared. Don't force anyone to give a lesson. Family meetings are meant to be enjoyable for everyone, even the person giving the lesson.

Lessons don't need to be long. Depending on the subject and the age of the person giving the lesson, a lesson might be only a couple of minutes. Lessons should be more than a lecture. Try to include questions that lead to discussions. As the parent, you might not agree with some of the opinions shared. That's okay. Do not argue. Family meeting lessons may lead to some serious one-on-one discussions with your children at a later time.

Here are some possible topics. Share them with your family and ask them what they think should be added to the list:

How to give a lesson
What to do in case of a fire
Good table manners
How to greet people
How to solve problems
When to use "I Feel" statements (explained in the chapter 16)
Stories of ancestors
Respect
Honesty and trust
Charity
Moral cleanliness
Peer pressure
Talking with strangers
What to do if offered drugs, alcohol or tobacco
Sexting
Gangs
What to do if someone wants you to participate in something illegal
Pornography
Bullying and Cyber bullying
Suicide

- Kindness
- Forgiveness
- Sacrifice
- The importance of education
- The importance of choosing good friends
- Being a good friend
- Gratitude
- The importance of physical exercise
- Healthy eating
- Service to others
- Dress, appearance and modesty
- The language we use
- How music affects us
- Budgeting money
- The importance of work

In her book, *350 Questions Parents Should Ask During Family Night*[1], Shannon Alder poses questions to get conversations started:

"What should you do if you see your friend being pressured to try drugs, alcohol, or cigarettes?"

"Your friend wants you to watch an R-rated movie, but you feel uncomfortable about it. What do you do?"

"You are alone in the house, and a stranger knocks at your door. The person says there has been an accident and they need to call 911. What do you do?"

You can't be there to protect your children all the time. But you can arm them with the knowledge they'll need to stay out of trouble, and a good training ground is weekly family meetings.

You might feel uncomfortable teaching some of the heavier topics. But remember this: your children will form opinions about all of these topics sometime during their early lives. Many of their opinions will be based on information they glean from the media (TV, movies, magazines, and the internet) and from people who are not concerned about their welfare. It will be easier for you to teach your kids before they are influenced by other sources. Helping to form young opinions can be a lot easier than trying to change their opinions later, and family meetings are the perfect place to do that.

Invite a Guest

Although most of your family meetings will involve only your family members, you can invite a guest to add a little variety to the gathering. Guests could come from extended family, such as grandparents, aunts, uncles, or cousins. Perhaps one of your children would like to include one of their friends in your family meeting. You could invite a friend or a neighbor to experience a family meeting. You could also invite an entire family to join you. Your family meeting might inspire others to start their own family meetings. Make sure there are enough treats to go around.

What if your lesson or Fun Time was directed by a *special guest*? That would definitely add some variety and create some fun anticipation. Ask Grandma to tell some stories about growing up in Ireland. Ask Grandpa to tell some of his army stories. Ask Aunt Hazel, who is famous for her delicious bread, to teach her secret recipe. Ask origami expert, Cousin Mike, to teach how to make a paper swan.

Do you know someone who would be good at teaching a lesson about drinking and using drugs, healthy eating, or budgeting money? Most people would feel flattered to be invited to teach something at your family meeting and your kids might pay more attention to a guest speaker than to you. Remember to give the guest speaker a time limit.

Keep a Record

If I could go back in time and change anything about the way we did family meetings, I would make sure someone wrote down what we discussed at every meeting. As I look over the scant records that were taken, I delight in reading them. I only wish there were more. So, don't make the mistake I did. From the first family meeting that you hold, take notes – write down a brief summary of discussion topics, decisions made, lessons taught, and what you did for Fun Time. Make sure each set of notes is signed, dated and kept in a safe place. Years later, you and your children will cherish the experience of looking back over them.

Assign Roles

After your family has settled into the routine of having regular family meetings, give your children the opportunity to become more involved by assigning roles: Meeting Leader, Record Keeper, Calendar Updater, Treat Server, Fun Time Planner, or Lesson Giver. All family members should have a role. Even very young children could pass out napkins to go with the treats. Rotate roles each week so everyone has a chance to participate in a different role. This will enable everyone to get involved and feel empowered.

There will be Bumps in the Road

Your aim should be to make family meetings enjoyable so everyone will want to come back the next week. Make sure to have

Fun Time at the end of every family meeting, even if it's only for a few minutes – even if it's the only thing you have time for.

With that said, be advised that some family meetings will not run smoothly. Some will be frustrating and some will be boring. One or more family members might come in a bad mood or be in a hurry to go somewhere. Arguments may erupt during your meeting. Do not get discouraged. Adjust if you have to. Don't let family meeting go too long. Make sure one person doesn't dominate the discussion. Don't wander off the agenda for too long. Turn cell phones off – hey, it's only for a few minutes!

Do your best to hold family meetings consistently. If you skip a week, just get back on track. You will find that family meetings are the best way to bring a family close together, and the best forum in which to teach problem-solving, decision-making and good family values. Some family meetings will be forgettable and some will be memorable. Some will be chaotic and some will be life-changing. The key is to keep trying.

6

Principle 3: Acknowledge Negative Feelings

All children have a need to feel heard and understood. You will meet this need by acknowledging negative feelings. When you acknowledge negative feelings, your children will be able to calm down, let go of their negative feelings, and often come up with ideas to solve the problem that caused their negative feelings. You will see positive results in seconds. When you acknowledge negative feelings on a regular basis, your children will feel more like approaching you when they have problems, even during the teenage years. Acknowledging negative feelings strengthens relationships.

In order to understand *acknowledging* negative feelings, it's helpful to first understand its opposite: *denying* negative feelings.

When a child says, "I hate Grandma!" what is a typical parent response?

"You don't hate Grandma, you love her," or, "I don't want to hear you talk like that, young man."

With these responses, the parent is denying the child's negative feelings or telling the child he is wrong to feel that way.

Here are some more examples of denying negative feelings:

Child: "I never want to see Emily again."
Parent: "Nonsense. You don't really mean that."

Child: "My teacher sucks."
Parent: "That's not a very nice thing to say."

Child: "I'm bored."
Parent: "Are you kidding - with all those toys?"

Parents who deny their children's negative feelings are not meeting their need to feel heard and understood. And when that need is not met, children become frustrated and angry. They can't let go of their negative feelings, so they suppress them. If this need continues to go unmet for a long time, the stored-up pain can result in defiance, depression, hostility and later, addictions.

Now let's contrast that with acknowledging negative feelings. Consider the following dialogue:

Child: "I hate Grandma!"
Parent: "Why do you say that?"
Child: "I just do."
Parent: "You sound mad."
Child: "She spends all the time with the baby."
Parent: "Oh, you wish she would spend more time with you."
Child: "Yes."

When children come to you in distress, they do not want you to agree, disagree, give your opinion, offer advice, or "fix" the problem. It is not the time to criticize by saying, "In our home, we don't say 'hate'," or "I think you're over reacting." What they want – and need – is for you to take a moment and give them your full attention. Then, listen to them and let them know you understand what they are *thinking* and what they are *feeling*.

When children come to you in distress, allow them to say whatever they want. Let them say all kinds of mean, nasty things, whether they are true or not. Permit them to vent. And while this is happening, let them feel heard and understood by acknowledging their negative feelings. If you grew up with your feelings frequently denied, you may find this principle challenging.

You may think that allowing your children to express their negative feelings will reinforce those feelings or cause those feelings to be expressed through bad behavior. This is simply not true. Actually, the opposite is true. When you allow your children to express their negative feelings, you are helping your children "let go" of those feelings. As a result, children will feel better and behave better.

Encouraging those angry feelings to come out also contributes to a stronger relationship, whereas trying to suppress those feelings can erode a relationship. Children who feel comfortable unloading on Mom and Dad early in their childhood will feel more like talking to them throughout their lives.

In their book, *How to talk so kids will Listen & Listen so kids will talk*[1], authors Adele Faber and Elaine Mazlish make what they call a tremendous discovery:

"The more you try to push a child's unhappy feelings away, the more he becomes stuck with them. The more comfortably you can accept the bad feelings, the easier it is for kids to let go of them. I guess you could say that if you want to have a happy family, you'd better be prepared to permit the expression of a lot of unhappiness."

There are two steps to acknowledging negative feelings:

1. Show that you are listening
2. Show that you understand.

Step 1. Show that you are listening. Make eye contact. Give your full attention. No multi-tasking. If your phone rings, ignore it or tell the caller that you'll call them back. Just listen and nod occasionally. By giving undivided attention, you let the child feel important and loved; something that contributes to his need for a sense of belonging.

Sometimes you don't even have to go to step 2. Often, when a child feels heard, he is able to let go of his anger or frustration, and that gives him the freedom to come up with a solution to his problem on his own. If you feel that listening alone is not enough to help the child feel better, then go to Step 2.

Step 2. Show that you understand. Showing that you understand has three options:

    a. Clarify – "Why would you say that?" or, "What happened?"
    b. Identify how the child is feeling – "That's gotta be frustrating," or simply, "Ohh noo."
    c. Reflect what the child is thinking – tell her what you think she's thinking.

Here are some examples. Notice that the parent does not judge, criticize, or try to tell the child that it's wrong to feel the way he does. Each dialogue has an example of clarifying, identifying how the child is feeling, and reflecting what the child is thinking. Experiment with these options until you get a feel for when it's best to use each one.

Child: "I'd like to punch that Michael in the nose."
Parent: "Why would you say that?" *(clarify.)*
Child: "He didn't invite me to his birthday party."
Parent: "Ohh noo," *(identify how the child is feeling.)* "You and Michael have been friends for a long time. You've got to wonder why he didn't invite you." *(Reflect what the child is thinking.)*

Child: "My teacher is stupid."
Parent: "What's going on?"

Child: "Just because of a little rain, she said we couldn't go on our field trip."
Parent: "Ohh noo. How disappointing."
Child: "I hate her."
Parent: "You've been looking forward to that field trip all week."

Child: "My life sucks!"
Parent: "Why would you say that?"
Child: "I don't get this math."
Parent: "That's gotta be frustrating."
Child: "You have no idea."
Parent: "You're usually good at figuring it out but now it's getting harder."

Child: "Mommy's mean."
Dad: "Why?"
Child: "She says I have to clean my room before we can go swimming."
Dad: "Oh, no."
Child: "Make her change her mind, can you, Dad?"
Dad: "You love to swim but you hate to clean."

As you practice using all three options in Step 2, you'll come to know just which options to use at the right time. When identifying the feeling, there are a lot of "feeling words" from which to choose. Here are some feeling words and their use in a sentence:

Tough – "That's got to be tough." (This is a good generic response to most negative feelings. You can also use, "Ohh noo.")

Shocking – "That must have been a shock."

Frustrating – "That must have been frustrating."

Discouraging – "How discouraging."

Angry – "You sound angry."

Mad – "You're THAT mad at him."

Annoying – "It's annoying to have to put up with that."

Disappointing – "That must have been disappointing."

Upset - "No wonder you're so upset."

Hurt - "Losing a friend can really hurt."

Scary - "The first day of school can be scary."

Unhappy - "You seem unhappy about something."

Embarrassing - "Being laughed at can be so embarrassing."

Hoping - "You were hoping to get it over with."

Doubt - "You're having doubts about going."

Sad - "Having a pet die is so sad."

Here are a few more examples of conversations when a child comes to Mom or Dad in distress. This time, each example will have two possible ways of handling the conversations. First, *denying* negative feelings, and then *acknowledging* negative feelings.

Denying negative feelings:

Child: "Jake is moving away."

Dad: "Don't worry, you have lots of friends. Plus, you can email Jake."

Child: "But it's not the same. We can't hang out together."

Dad: "Well, life is tough, Son. Sometimes bad things happen."

Child: "You don't get it, Dad. I'll never have a friend like that again."

Dad: "You might think so now, but down the road you'll make new friends to hang out with and probably even forget about Jake."

Child: "Never mind, I'm outta here."

Acknowledging negative feelings:

Child: "Jake is moving away."
Dad: "Oh no. What a shock."
Child: "We'll never be able to hang out together."
Dad: "You two are best friends. That's got to be tough."
Child: "I'll never have another friend like him, ever."
Dad: "Mmm."
Child: "It's like we can read each other's mind. We know what the other is going to say."
Dad: "And now he's moving. That's sad."
Child: "I guess there's always email, skype, and I could go visit him, right?"

You may feel that verbalizing a feeling will make it worse. Just the opposite is true. When a child hears the words that identify what he is feeling, he feels comforted. Don't worry about choosing the wrong emotion. If you do, your child will correct you:

"You must feel angry."

"Not so much angry as I am disappointed that I can't trust her anymore."

"I see."

Denying negative feelings:

Child: "I'm not cleaning my room."
Mom: "And why not?"
Child: "Because."

Mom: "Well, I'm sorry, but you should have thought about that when you made the mess."

Child:*(Starts crying.)*

Mom: "Now go up there and get started."

Child: *(Sits on the floor, folds her arms and cries louder.)*

Mom: *(Grabs her arm and takes her to her room.)* "Now don't come out until this room is clean. Do you understand?"

Child*: (Continues crying.)* "But why, Mom?"

Mom: "Because I said so!"

Acknowledging negative feelings:

Child: "I'm not cleaning my room."

Mom: "Oh?"

Child: *(Is silent)*

Mom: *(Is silent but turns her whole attention to the child. Nods as if to say, "You have my attention, go on.")*

Child: "I'm not cleaning my room."

Mom: "Sounds to me like you're upset."

Child: "I'm not cleaning my room."

Mom: "I see. You really sound mad."

Child: *(Starts to cry.)* "There's too much."

Mom: "Oooh. There's such a big mess that you're discouraged, like it might take you forever."

Child: "It will."

Mom: "Hmm."

Child: *(Crying)*

Mom: *(Is silent)*

Child: "Can you help me?"

Mom: "I'll tell you what. I'll help you clean for one minute. We will both clean as fast as we can. I mean super-hero fast. Then I'll leave you to finish."

Child: "Okay, Mom." *(Takes mom's hand and pulls her toward the bedroom.)*

Hold off on giving advice or solving the problem.

This mom could have said, "Would you like me to help you?" But that would have taken away the learning opportunity for the child to solve the problem herself. If the child never got around to asking for help, then it would have been reasonable for Mom to ask if she could help.

What if Mom cannot help? If Mom does nothing more than acknowledge her daughter's bad feelings about cleaning, her daughter will feel heard and understood, and that will make cleaning feel a little easier – we hope. After the child has finished cleaning her room to Mom's satisfaction, Mom can take advantage of a teaching opportunity:

Mom: "How do you feel now that your room is done?"
Child: "Good."
Mom: "How did you feel before you started cleaning?"
Child: "Bad."
Mom: "Will I always be able to help you clean your room?"
Child: "Probably not."
Mom: "So what can you do so you don't feel so bad about cleaning your room?"
Child: "I don't know."
Mom: "Think hard."
Child: "Maybe not let it get so messy?"
Mom: "Good answer. I think you've got it. High five." *(Mom and daughter high five each other.)*

By now you've probably guessed that dealing with feelings is more of an art than a science. This new "responding skill" can feel awkward at first. You will go through some trial and error. The important thing is that you keep trying, because if you give up and revert back to your old habits of denying negative feelings, your child might turn to someone else for understanding, and that someone else may not have your child's best interest at heart. Here's one more example:

Dad: "Hi son. How was your day?"
Son: "It sucked! And I don't want to talk about it."
Dad: "That bad, huh?"
Son: "It was terrible."
Dad: "Why? What happened?"
Son: "The coach posted a list of everyone who made the team. I wasn't on it. I was cut from the team. I thought I'd be first string. I didn't even make second string and I'm better than most of the guys that tried out."

Dad's initial reaction is to say, "I told you that you should practice more but you didn't listen to me." Instead, he decides to acknowledge negative feelings.

Dad: "You were cut from the team? Oh my gosh."
Son: "That's not the worst of it. Mike and Joe made the cut. They're on the team and I'm not. They're going to be at practice while I'm going to be... I don't know. I hate it!"
Dad: "Hmmm."

Dad will keep listening until his son has had time to vent. He'll refrain from criticizing or giving his opinion. He will show that he is listening and show that he understands. His son already knows he should have practiced more and is now paying for it. He just needs his dad to listen to him.

What if you notice your child is sad or upset about something? How would you initiate the conversation? I'm going to suggest against saying, "What's eating you?" Instead, I'm going to recommend something better. Describe what you see. "*I see something is making you sad.*" Or, "*you seem* upset. Would you like to talk about it?"

One day my 4-year-old-granddaughter, Brooklyn, and her little brother, Stockton, were visiting. In my family room is the "spinning chair." It's an office chair that they love to spin around on. They both saw the chair at the same time and made a bee-line for it. Little brother won the race and climbed up in the chair. I could see Brooklyn starting to look mad and I was afraid she might hit Stockton out of frustration.

My first thought was to say, "Brooklyn. Stockton beat you fair and square. Now, you just wait for him to have a turn and then it will be your turn."

Instead, I decided to acknowledge her negative feelings.

I knelt down on one knee, so I was eye-to-eye with her, and said, "Brooklyn, you are mad. You wanted to beat Stockton to that chair and I think you wanted him to spin you around."

She didn't say a word, but I could see her whole body relax. She turned around and off she went. Acknowledging negative feelings is a powerful way to help children let go of their negative feelings.

I think you'll discover, as I did, that you will have many opportunities to acknowledge negative feelings, and this skill will become one of your favorites.

Empathy

You may know Acknowledging Negative Feelings by a different name: empathy.

Empathy is getting into another person's head; experiencing the feelings of another person. If they hurt, you hurt.

Empathy is sharing someone's emotional pain, and helping her to feel that she does not have to experience all that pain alone.

Empathy is taking all the big, messy emotions and putting them into words to make them more understandable and thereby more manageable.

Empathy says, what you're feeling matters to me. I'm interested and I care.

Empathy provides healing. It is more life-changing (and behavior changing) than logic.

Empathy is the most powerful and effective way for two people to connect.

When you offer empathy to children who are feeling hurt, sad, angry, frustrated, or embarrassed, you give them the gift of being heard and understood. And that can be like throwing a life preserver to someone who is emotionally drowning.

When you help your children experience empathy, you also help them to develop empathy for others.

When a child comes to you in destress, resist the urge to:

Fix the problem
Offer advice
Agree
Disagree
Give your opinion

Instead:

Listen
Clarify
Identify how the other person is feeling

Reflect what the other person is thinking

When I learn of another school shooting, hear of another suicide, or think about the millions of people caught up in drug addiction, I wonder if some of these situations could have been prevented if these people had experienced more empathy when they were growing up. Then I wonder how many children are on a path to destructive behavior right now, whose lives can be turned around with empathy. Empathy is the power to change lives. When you acknowledge your children's negative feelings, you are applying empathy. There is no substitute for empathy. There is no experience or physical gift that will have as great an impact on a child in distress as empathy.

Give in Fantasy

Give in fantasy what you cannot give in reality. Do you have memories of wanting something badly and getting a logical explanation about why you couldn't have it? It didn't make you feel one bit better, did it? We often do the same to our own children. When they want something they can't have, we think that giving reasons and logical explanations will cause them to stop asking, like in this example: Lily is sitting down for breakfast.

Lily: "I want frosty flakes, Mom."

Mom: "I'm sorry, Honey, we're out."

Lily: "I want frosty flakes!" She starts to kick her legs.

Mom: "Quit whining. We don't have any. You'll have to eat something else."

Lily: "But I want frosty flakes!" She starts to cry.

Mom: "Stop being unreasonable. There's nothing I can do about it."

Lily: (Starts to go into a meltdown.)

Logical explanations do not console an emotionally driven child. What can you do instead? Give your child in fantasy what she cannot have in reality.

Lily: "I want frosty flakes, Mom."

Mom: I'm sorry, Honey, we're out."

Lily: "I want frosty flakes!" She starts to kick her legs.

Mom: "I hear you. You really wish you had a big bowl of frosty flakes."

Lily: "Yes."

Mom: "A giant bowl. Would you want bananas or raisins on top?"

Lily: "Both."

Mom: "Both it is. And we'll top it off with some milk. Now, I have these two cereals. You choose. Which do you want?"

When you give a child in fantasy what you cannot give in reality, you are acknowledging her negative feelings, and she is more able to deal with reality. In the small amount of time it takes to give in fantasy, the child feels understood, and when the child feels understood, she tends to calm down.

Billy and Mom were at the toy store to select a gift for a birthday party. Mom turned around to see Billy holding a box containing a remote control car.

Billy: "Mom. Can we buy this?"

Mom: "That looks like fun. You wish you could take it home."

Billy: "Yeah, can we, Mom?"

Mom: "I wish I could buy that right now, but I can't."

Billy, feeling disappointed, put the car back, but felt like mom understood how he felt.

Granting in fantasy works with adults too. Mom was admiring a dress at a clothing store. Dad approached her. Here are two different ways he could talk to her.

Way 1. "Don't even think about it. You know that's way out of our budget. You shouldn't even be looking at dresses like that. It only sets you up for disappointment."

Way 2: "I can see you in that dress. With the right accessories you would look pretty amazing. I would be proud to escort you anywhere."

Which way would get Dad his favorite meal tonight?

7

Principle 4: Get to Know Your Kids

Each one of your children have likes, dislikes, opinions, worries, desires, fears, wishes and beliefs, whether you know about them or not. If your children feel they can talk to you about these things and feel safe when sharing them with you, your relationship with them will strengthen, trust will grow, and cooperation will improve. So how do you get them to open up? By asking questions, listening, and refraining from criticizing. By doing so, you will be giving them the positive attention they crave and meeting their need for a sense of belonging.

But be warned. If they feel any criticism, even the slightest bit, they will shut down and quit sharing their feelings with you for days, months, or even years.

Good times to ask questions would be while peeling potatoes together, eating together, riding in the car together, spending one-on-one time together, or during family meetings. "So, what is one good thing that happened to you today?" Questions get people thinking and interesting conversations can result.

Remember, no criticizing. Just listen and try to understand. Here is a list of possible questions to get you started. I'll bet you will be surprised and amazed at what your children think about various subjects.

1. If you could do anything you wanted, what would that be?

2. What was the hardest thing you did today?
3. What is the hardest thing you have ever done?
4. What is the bravest thing you've done?
5. What is something that makes you laugh?
6. If you could be any animal, what would you be?
7. If you could visit any place, where would that be?"
8. Tell us one thing that you like about the person on your left.
9. What is something that you worry about?
10. What do you like about Dad?
11. What do you like about Mom?
12. If you could change anything about Dad, what would it be?
13. If you could change anything about Mom, what would it be?
14. What is the thing you like best about our home?
15. If you could change anything about our home, what would it be?
16. What food do you love, and what food do you hate?
17. If you could have any three wishes, what would they be?
18. If you won a million dollars, what would you do?
19. What is the one chore that you hate the most?
20. If someone asked you to suggest a name for their new baby, what would it be?
21. What are you the most thankful for?
22. Know any good jokes?
23. Which do you like better, cats or dogs?
24. What skill would you like to learn?
25. If you found a $100 bill, what would you do with it?
26. If you could have a super power, what would it be?
27. What do you like to do for fun?
28. What do you want to be when you grow up?

29. What is the best thing about being *(insert child's name here)*?
30. Who is your favorite singer?
31. What is the nicest thing any has ever done for you?
32. What is your favorite thing to do in school?
33. What is your favorite dessert?
34. What is your favorite flavor of ice cream?
35. What is your favorite season?
36. What is your favorite song?
37. What is your favorite game?
38. What is your favorite holiday?
39. What is your favorite video game?
40. Where is your favorite place to eat out?
41. What is your favorite car?
42. Who is your favorite sports player?
43. If you could play any musical instrument, what would it be?
44. What is something fun you'd like to do this summer?
45. What is one thing you'd like to learn to do?
46. What makes a good friend?
47. If you could spend the day with anyone, who would that be?
48. What are you most afraid of?
49. What is your dream vacation if money were no object?
50. What is your favorite book?
51. Have you ever done something you regret?
52. What is something you really like about yourself?
53. What do you think one of your best qualities is?
54. What makes people likable?
55. Is there a person who has inspired you?
56. What do you think our family motto should be?

57. If you could start a new family tradition, what would it be?
58. What's something you've really worked hard for?
59. What's one goal you'd like to accomplish this year?
60. What is the best part about summer? Winter?
61. What is something we can do better as a family?
62. Do we have a family rule that you think is unfair?
63. Is there a new rule you thing our family should adopt?
64. What is one word that describes our family?
65. What is your most memorable Christmas?
66. What is one fear you would like to conquer?
67. What age would you like to be right now and why?
68. When you do something hard, what keeps you from quitting?
69. If you were a Dad (or Mom), what would you do differently?
70. Describe your dream home.
71. If you could go back in time to see something, what would that be?
72. If you could go back in time and change something, what would that be?
73. A time I will never forget is _____?
74. How would your life be different if you had no fear?
75. What is love?
76. How do you deal with people you can't trust?
77. How do you know when you can trust someone?
78. Is it ever okay to break a promise?
79. Is it ever okay to tell a lie?
80. Have you ever had trouble forgiving someone?
81. What do you like better, the mountains or the beach?
82. What do you do when you can't fall asleep?
83. What is something you will never do again?

84. If you could be really good at something, what would it be?
85. What makes you angry?
86. What makes you happy?
87. What is an embarrassing experience you've had?
88. What would you do if money were no object?
89. What country would you like to visit?
90. What other language would you like to speak?
91. Do you believe in God?
92. How do you feel when you are home alone?
93. What is something you would change about yourself?
94. How do you decide between right and wrong?
95. How do you handle disappointment or failure?
96. What experience has taught you the most?
97. What are the three most important things in your life?
98. If you were to plan a party, what would you do?
99. Do you learn more when you succeed or fail? Why?
100. What do you like about being a boy? Girl?
101. What is the worst job you can think of?
102. What is the one thing you can't live without?
103. What is one rule that you live by?
104. What is one question you'd like answered about the future?
105. What do you want to be remembered for?
106. What is your biggest pet peeve?
107. What would you do if you saw someone making fun of someone else?
108. What do children know more about than adults?
109. What is your favorite thing to do for exercise?
110. What is your earliest memory?
111. What one thing would you grab if the house was on fire?
112. What is the greatest invention of all time?

113. If the electricity went out for a week, how would that affect you?

114. What is something you have never done that you would like to try?

115. If you knew you couldn't fail, what would you do?

116. If you knew you could do anything, even if it meant failing a few times, what would you do?

8

Principle 5: Make Positive Deposits

In his book, *The 7 Habits of Highly Effective Families*[1], Stephen R. Covey teaches how you can improve relationships with your children by using the analogy of an emotional bank account. By doing things that build trust in your relationship, you make deposits. By doing things that decrease the level of trust in your relationship, you make withdrawals. Examples of making withdrawals would be nagging, criticizing, and losing your temper.

If you have a high, positive balance in this emotional bank account, the level of trust is high, and communication is open and free and your ability to influence another person is increased dramatically. If you have a low balance or are overdrawn, there is little or no trust, no real communication, and your ability to influence another person is decreased considerably. Here are 10 deposits you can make in your children's Emotional Bank Accounts.

1. Be Thoughtful

It's the little things that make a big difference. Saying cutting or sarcastic remarks is a withdrawal. Words like, *please, thank you, excuse me, may I help you, after you*, and *you look nice*, are emotional deposits. Other deposits include doing small favors, calling just to say, "Hi," expressing appreciation, and giving sincere compliments. Tucking a note in a lunch box, writing a kind note on a mirror, fixing a favorite breakfast, and giving a hug or even a smile are ways of making deposits.

2. Use Hello and Goodbye to Show You Care

Always take advantage of the opportunity to greet your children when you haven't seen them for a while. This gives them a boost of positive attention and meets their need for a sense of belonging in a positive way. Imagine you are a child, and when Dad comes home from work, one of the first things he does is find you to say, "Hello." Wouldn't that make you feel important? You can have the same positive effect on your children. What if you made sure to say goodbye to each child before you left to go somewhere? Another positive deposit. Don't forget to make children feel important when they go to bed at night by saying good night and giving a hug and an, "I love you." Then in the morning when you first see them, greet each like they were an important person: "Good morning. How did you sleep?" All these positive deposits will add up to strengthen your relationships.

3. Apologize when necessary

Some parents think that apologizing is a sign of weakness, when in fact, just the opposite is true. Apologizing turns withdrawals into deposits. "I said some things that were unkind and I want to apologize. I was angry and upset, but I should not have said what I did." We all make mistakes. When we do, we need to own up to it, sincerely apologize, and move on. The outcome will be far better than trying to hold on to stubborn pride.

4. Keep Promises

Making and breaking a promise is a huge withdrawal. Promises create excitement, anticipation and trust. Broken promises create disappointment and mistrust. It is better not to make a promise than to make one and break it. On the other hand, making and keeping promises are huge emotional deposits. If you make a promise to a child, do everything in your power to see it through.

5. Forgive

Your children will give you multiple opportunities every day to practice forgiveness. Forgiveness will free you from the burden that anger places on you. It releases bitterness and resentment you feel when your children are inconsiderate, uncooperative, rude, disrespectful and rebellious. Never stop forgiving.

6. Laugh Together

Besides strengthening your immune system, boosting your energy, and reducing stress, laughing together with your kids is a good bonding activity and an emotional deposit. Kids like being with you when you make them feel good and laughing makes them (and you) feel good. Laughing with your children:

Strengthens your relationship and promotes bonding
Allows your children to express their deeply felt emotions more freely
Gives your children a good dose of acceptance and a sense of belonging
Helps you and your children let go of anger and resentment
Makes parenting fun

Makes being a kid fun

If there was a pill that provided all the benefits of laughter, it would be in very high demand. Ask your kids if anything funny happened to them today. A good time to do this is at the dinner table, at family meetings, or after they've climbed into bed at night.

Of course it goes without saying that laughter must be shared by everyone. If someone is the brunt of a joke or the object of sarcasm, then your laughter takes on the form of a major emotional withdrawal and harms your relationship – even if you say, "Just kidding."

7. Touch in Gentle and Loving Ways

Appropriate touching can be a powerful way to increase bonding, cooperation, and teamwork within our families. Babies actually need loving touch to develop properly, both physically and emotionally. As children grow, it can be hard to maintain a culture of touching, so here are some suggestions to get in the habit of touching.

> Give hugs every day. Make a routine out of hugging your children when they get up, when they're leaving for school, when they get home, and before bed. A hug is a way to share both good and bad times. A hug can create a connection that words alone cannot.

> Children love to cuddle. Pile the whole family on the couch to watch TV instead of sitting in separate chairs. Cuddle together for bedtime stories.

> Use touch from time to time when listening, when celebrating an accomplishment, or giving attention to good behavior. You

can do a touch on the arm, a pat on the back, a fist bump, a high-five, or a hug.

Offer your hand to help someone up off the floor.

If you see someone coming up the stairs, offer your hand to help them up the last couple of steps.

8. Reading Together

Studies have shown that reading to your children helps them develop language skills, problem-solving skills, creativity and empathy. When they go to school, they tend to do better. Reading to children will bring the two of you closer together. You can start reading to children before they're even able to say words. As they learn to read, you can take turns reading. This is a good way for children to feel a positive sense of belonging, and a huge deposit in their emotional bank account. All you need is a library card - and it's free.

9. Say I Love You

Some parents have a hard time saying, "I love you" to their children. Here are some things that happen to children when they hear "I love you." It makes them feel valuable. It gives them the freedom to make mistakes. It gives them confidence. It gives them courage. It helps them to love others. It creates a desire to love you back. You're missing an opportunity to make significant emotional deposits if you don't tell your children you love them every day

10. Treat Your Spouse with Respect and Kindness

From the time your children are very young, they notice and remember how Mom and Dad treat each other. Not only do they notice, they copy it. If Mom and Dad treat each other with kindness and respect, there's a higher chance the children will treat each other with kindness and respect. If parents use belittling comments, swearing, verbal abuse, yelling, harsh criticism, sarcastic remarks, verbal threats, slamming doors, unwanted physical contact, arguing, rudeness, or disrespect even by one parent, you can bet it will have dramatic negative effect on the children. One of the best ways you and your spouse can make positive deposits into your children's emotional bank account is to show respect, kindness, and love toward each other.

Section 2

Teach Children Life Skills, Good Values, and Desirable Behavior

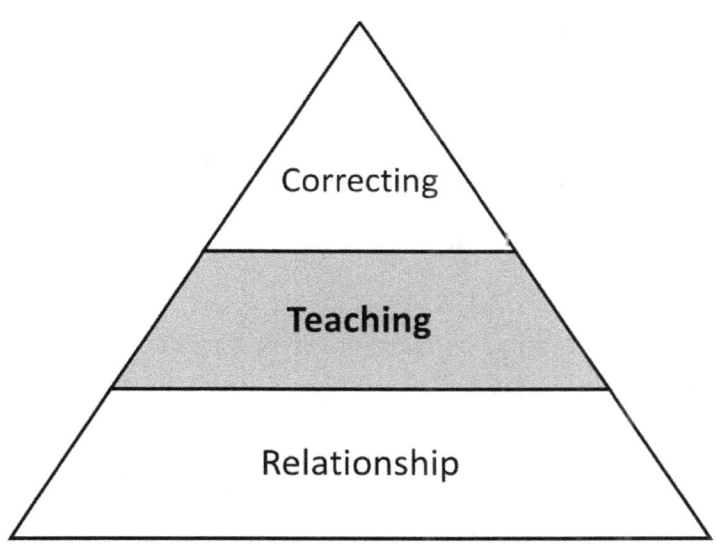

When your child fails to behave properly, imagine that she is trying to tell you two things:

1. "I want a better relationship with you." Section 1 focuses on strengthening relationships. In order for children to be receptive to your teaching, it's necessary to have a good relationship with them.

2. "I need you to teach me how you expect me to behave." This section focuses on teaching. I have divided teaching into two categories: *direct teaching* and *indirect teaching*. Direct teaching is when you:

> Teach life skills
> Teach good values
> Teach desirable behavior

Indirect teaching is when you:

> Model good behavior
> Give attention to good behavior
> Offer choices

Misbehavior should be recognized as a reason to teach, not as an excuse to punish. When a child behaves badly, rather than say, "That child needs to be punished," say, "That child hasn't learned proper behavior." A child must know what is expected of him and then be *willing* to comply. The willingness to comply is determined by the strength of the connection he has with you. The stronger the connection, the more willing he is to comply. The weaker the connection, the less he cares.

9

Teach Life Skills

As a parent, what is it that you want to ultimately accomplish? My guess is that you want to see to it that your child learns to become an independent adult, with the knowledge and ability to take good care of him or herself when the time comes to leave the nest. As your child progresses, you will take pleasure in watching and participating in each accomplishment along the way. Shouldn't that be the goal of every parent?

As important as that goal seems to be, it is my observation that many young adults are incapable of taking care of themselves because they have not been trained. Instead, their parents do everything for them and deny them learning opportunities that would help them become independent, happy adults.

I see two reasons for this. 1) Parents feel that the way to communicate love for their children is by doing everything for their children; things that their children could be doing on their own. 2) Parents get worn down by the whining and complaining and feel it is just easier to do things for their children, rather than make them do it themselves. In both cases, the parents are focusing on the moment, and not on the big picture.

In her book, *The Parenting Breakthrough*[1], Merrilee Brown Boyack talks about over-nurturing children. She says, "Parents who nurture too much convey messages like these to their children: You can't do this because:

> You're not smart enough
> You're not reliable enough
> You're not old enough
> You're not responsible enough
> You're *just* a child
> I don't trust you
> I don't believe in you
> You're not capable of taking care of yourself
> The quality of your work is inadequate
> Only women do these kinds of things
> Only men do these kinds of things
>
> Moms do all the dirty work. (Conveying a serious lack of respect for women)"

Contrast this with parents who keep their children's future in mind. They love their children and want them to be happy, but rather than doing everything for them, they train their children in age-related skills and watch their children learn, struggle, make mistakes, figure it out and eventually thrive as they master those skills. They watch their children's self-esteem grow as they take on the belief that *I can do this myself.* They watch their children's self-confidence grow as their children take steps to become capable and independent.

Children lack vision. That's why they have parents. Your role as a parent is to take charge and be a leader. Your role is to train your children to be independent adults someday, and give you grandchildren. Then you can spoil all you want because that's what grandparents do. But until then, you need to give your children the knowledge and ability to succeed in a tough world.

As a take-charge parent (or the boss of your kids), you are going to experience frustration as your children resist and ask, "But why do I have to?" You will look them in the eye and say, "Because I have more information and experience than you do and I know what you're going to be up against when you strike out on your own. So, you can take comfort in knowing that I will do everything I can to get you prepared."

Your children don't know it, but you are going to give them a gift that will benefit them for the rest of their lives: the gift of knowledge and ability; the gift of independence.

Life skills are skills that help children make the transition from dependence to independence by adding to their capabilities. From putting toys in the toy box to mowing the lawn, life skills prepare a child to be productive. When you teach children life skills you empower them. You give them the ability, the confidence, and the *power* to do something they couldn't do before. There are many benefits of empowering your children. They would include:

It instills in them a sense of accomplishment and confidence.

It enables them to be a more capable, contributing member of the family, thus satisfying their need to feel a sense of belonging.

It increases their sense of personal power so they don't feel they have to be sassy or defiant to meet that need on their own.

It helps them to become more independent.

It prepares them to be a productive member of society.

It gives them skills they will need as adults.

It could begin an interest in something that turns into a passion.

They learn at a younger age with your help than they would without your help.

It strengthens the connection between child and parent.

The more they learn to do, the less Mom and Dad have to do for them.

It increases good behavior and decreases bad behavior.

Life skills include household responsibilities, but go beyond that. They include anything that enriches someone's life, such as learning to count, throwing a ball, riding a bike, making a healthy smoothie, learning to swim, or riding a horse. As children are exposed to life skills, they will decide what interests them and what doesn't.

Keep in mind that what interests you may not necessarily interest them. And what interests one child might not interest another. Exposing them to many life skills will give them opportunities to *choose* what they like and what they don't like, and being able to *choose* helps satisfy their need for a sense of personal power.

As mentioned throughout this book, children are hard-wired with a need for a sense of belonging and personal power. Teaching them life skills is a good way to satisfy both needs in positive ways. You can give them a sense of belonging by spending time teaching them. You can give them a sense of personal power by empowering them with new skills.

I believe every child is born with unique talents and gifts, and the more you expose your children to new life skills, the greater the chance those unique gifts will be discovered. For example, a child may be born with the gift of singing. But unless that child is exposed to opportunities to sing, that gift may never be realized.

Sometimes parents don't attempt to train their children to do something because it's faster, less frustrating, and done better if they just do it themselves. But then both the children and the parents lose out on the benefits of empowerment.

Four-year-old Tyler tried pouring milk from a gallon plastic jug and poured more on the table than in his cup.

He looked at Dad, fearful of being scolded.

"That's okay," said Dad, "let's clean it up together."

Dad got a sponge and started to mop up the milk.

"Here, use this," he said, handing Tyler the sponge.

Tyler finished sponging up the mess.

"I have an idea," said Dad, "let's play the pouring game."

He found a pitcher and poured the remaining milk from the jug into the pitcher and put the pitcher in the refrigerator. Then he rinsed out the jug and put an inch of water in it. He took the jug and a cup over to the table.

"I want you to pour this water into this cup." Dad said to Tyler.

The jug was light and Tyler had little trouble as he slowly poured.

"Hey, you did it!" said Dad. "Now let's put a little more water in the jug and try it again."

He filled the jug up half way with water.

"Don't worry about spilling," Dad said, "after all, this is the pouring game and it's okay if you spill. Let's see how you do."

Tyler picked up the jug and tipped it. Water spilled all over the table.

"That was a good try," said Dad. "Try again."

Tyler practiced. Dad emptied his cup and Tyler practiced some more. Dad told him how he was getting better. Then Dad filled the jug to the top and gave it to Tyler. It was heavy now. He learned to tip the jug without picking it up. Each time he practiced, he learned a little more about pouring.

The pouring game was also a good way for Dad to teach Tyler that it was okay to try and fail. When you fail, you learn. Each time Tyler got a little better at pouring, he felt more confident. He couldn't wait to show Mom.

As Tyler learns new things, his confidence grows. As his confidence grows, he becomes less afraid and more eager to learn more new things. As he learns more things, he develops a desire to learn harder things that require more effort and patience. The earlier he starts, the more he learns before he leaves the nest.

The Training Plan

Imagine sending your child into the world knowing how to do such things as shop for food, cook, pay bills, change a flat tire, do laundry, iron clothes, wash dishes, clean the oven, budget money, understand debit and credit cards, make repairs, vote, sell items on the internet, mend clothing, properly treat a spouse, raise a family, and make a living. All these adult skills start with learning important life-skills at a young age – such skills as dressing oneself, picking up toys, setting the table, making one's own lunch, emptying the dishwasher, baking cookies, and checking the oil in the car. You will not have to worry about your child leaving home with crucial gaps in experience and knowledge that would prevent him or her from having a successful adult life. Your children will be forever grateful for your efforts, and your legacy will continue through generations.

Let's make a list of life skills you can teach your children. The following will get you started. What can you add to the list?

Ages 2-3
- Put away toys
- Get dressed
- Put dirty clothes in the hamper
- Take plates to kitchen sink after eating
- Set the table with help
- Begin to brush teeth
- Carry in the mail
- Wash and dry hands – with the help of a stool
- Put clean silverware away
- Count to 10
- Kick a soft, inflatable ball
- Say "Please," and, "Thank you"
- Stay away from the street
- Cross the street safely with an adult

Ages 4-5
- Tie shoes
- Recite full name, address and phone number
- What to do if a stranger engages you
- What to do if there is a fire
- Use the phone
- Make a 911 call
- Clear the dinner table and wipe it down after a meal
- Put toys away when done playing with them
- Feed the family pet
- Set the table independently
- Fold towels
- Brush teeth and comb hair without assistance
- Water plants
- Help vacuum

Use good table manners
Ride a bike – wear a bike helmet
Count to 100
Read
Tell time
Make a paper airplane
Draw a picture

Ages 6-7
Make a sandwich
Rinse, dry, and put dishes away
Empty the dishwasher
Make the bed
Vacuum without help
Use an alarm to get up in the morning
Bathe him/herself, dry off with a towel, hang the towel up
Take a shower
Pump up a bicycle tire
Properly greet an adult
Shake hands (with a firm grip)
Count money
Change a light bulb
Run the microwave
Wrap a present
Do homework without constant supervision
Play simple board games
Throw a ball and catch with a mitt – underhanded at close range
Whistle
Arithmetic
Origami

Tie a knot
Begin piano lessons
Skip flat stones on a lake

Ages 8-9

Wash the dishes or fill the dishwasher
Fold clothes and put them away
Use a broom and dustpan
Clean a toilet
Mop the floor
Take the trash out
Make a simple meal, like macaroni and cheese
Make cookies from a box
Plant, water and weed a garden
Fish
Wash and vacuum a car
Order for yourself at a restaurant
Knit a scarf
Perform a simple magic trick
Have a savings account
Use email
Write and send letters
Learn the dangers of alcohol, drugs and tobacco and what to do when offered

Ages 10-13

Use the internet (with a filter)
Use a sewing machine
Change bed sheets
Plunge a toilet
Make bread
Understand basic nutrition

Understand weight control

Use the washing machine and dryer

Use a newspaper and flyers to find bargains and coupons

Shop for food

Prepare meals and desserts from a recipe book

Learn meat handling rules and food handling basics

Iron clothes

Tie a necktie

Hammer nails

Use power tools

Mow the lawn

Use a weed whacker

Paint a wall

Take the Red Cross babysitting course

Learn first aid – certify for CPR

Babysit with an adult nearby

Be able to apply practical math skills

Wardrobe matching

Make and keep dentist appointments

Juggling

Yo-yo-ing

Hula hooping

Type without looking

Budget money

Pay household bills

Understand debit and credit cards, interest and debt

Order something on the internet

Sell something on the internet

Understand prescriptions

Start to learn computer programs, like Microsoft Word and Excel

Ages 14-16
- Learn basic household repairs
- Memorize Social Security Number
- Accompany parent to vote
- Accompany parent to register a car
- Learn how car insurance works
- Change a flat tire
- Jumpstart a car
- Check tire pressure and oil in a car and top off windshield fluid
- Understand a car's maintenance schedule
- Understand what a car's warning lights mean
- Perform thorough car detailing
- Learn the rules of the road
- Learn to drive
- Learn about hair, makeup, jewelry, fingernail painting (girls)
- Create a resume, cover letter, and learn how to interview
- Open a bank account

Incredible, isn't it? Not until you sit down and make a list do you realize how much someone needs to know to be a successful, independent adult; and there's so much more that can be added to the list depending on your family. Your list might even inspire *you* to learn something new. Hey, it's never too late! Go over this list with your spouse to see what else needs to be included.

Okay, you've got this massive list and you're feeling totally overwhelmed. You were just coming to terms with spending daily personal time with each of your children, having weekly family meetings, and now this. Don't worry. You will be amazed at how well this fits into your family schedule and the benefits you will receive by having your children trained in these life skills.

Putting the Training Plan into Action

You will do most of the training, but you do not have to do all the training. Training can also come from an older sibling, an aunt, uncle, trusted friend, or a Boy Scout or Girl Scout troop. Whoever it is, you are still responsible for the training to be done right, so you need to be sure the child is learning what you expect.

Who do you know who could teach your child how to take care of a bicycle? Can an older sibling teach a younger sibling how to tie shoes? Do you have a soccer player friend who can teach your child the ins and outs of kicking and passing? Can Grandma teach how to plant a garden? Can Grandpa teach how to catch a fish? Can you go to a teacher or a scout leader and ask that they teach a lesson on table manners? Can Aunt Christine teach how to change a tire? Yes, there is nothing more effective in crushing a stereotype than a girl teaching "guy stuff" and a guy teaching "girl stuff." Can Dad teach how to make chocolate chip cookies?

Do you have a child who could teach their younger bother the finer points of cleaning the toilet? Boys who learn to clean the toilet are inclined to aim more accurately, knowing they will have to clean later.

Ensure your child's safety. Make sure the person you ask to train your child is someone you know and trust, and that your child will never be alone with that person.

Remember that this is training and kids will make mistakes. *Do not criticize imperfection.* Be patient. You may be a pro at a particular life skill, but your child is new at it and will want to withdraw if she feels that you are impatient.

Instead of saying, "That's not how I taught you to make your bed," say, "good effort on the bed. I notice you got the wrinkles out, but what could you do to make this bedspread a little straighter?"

Point out what they did well ("I notice you got the wrinkles out") and then *ask* what they could do make a specific improvement ("but what could you do to make this bedspread a little straighter?").

When you ask instead of tell, it helps your child develop problem-solving skills. If the child doesn't know the answer to the question, you can say, "May I make a suggestion?" If the child really messes up, say, "That's okay. You're just learning. It's okay to mess up. Keep trying. You'll get it with a little more practice."

Now if a child has been practicing a skill for a while and starts to get lazy or doesn't meet expectations, refrain from criticizing: "Son, that's not how I trained you to wash clothes. What's the matter with you?" Instead, go back to teaching mode and say, "Son, remember when I taught you about doing laundry? Do you remember what I said about separating colors?" (Let child respond) "And why do you suppose I told you that?" Don't criticize. Instead, ask questions.

Some training only takes a couple of minutes, like teaching a child how to handle a stranger at the door when Mom and Dad are gone: Knock knock. "Shhh. Don't make a sound. Don't open the door." Boom. Done.

Teach a child to feed the dog: Scoop out the food with a cup. Fill the water bowl half way. Done – and you are on your way to empowering your children and reaping the benefits.

Once children learn a new skill, have them take responsibility for it. Let them make the skill a part of their lives. Don't do it for them. Once they've learned to dress themselves, tie their shoes, feed the pet, do dishes, clean their bedroom, pick out their clothes, wash their clothes, iron their clothes, or fix snacks, let them. Many of their new skills will turn into daily or weekly chores. Then, if you occasionally decide to do something for the child that he has mastered, you'll be doing it out of kindness, love and caring.

Teaching children life skills might seem like a lot of work, but in the long run, the rewards will be worth it. No longer will your children run to you with an urgent request, "Mom, can you hurry and wash this?" or "Can you iron this for me?" or "I'm hungry. Can you make me a snack?" Your children will know how to wash and iron their clothes and fix snacks and meals. Their self-esteem will be a reflection of their self-sufficiency. They will learn how consequences are a result of their actions or in-actions. And when the time comes, they will be better prepared for the workforce and a family of their own.

Children love to help at a young age. Take advantage of that. Have your child help you with a recipe by cracking an egg into a bowl. Have him help you take out the garbage by holding on to the garbage bag while you both take it out to the trash can. Have him help sweep the floor by holding the dust pan. When a child says, "Can I try that?" Consider making that a teaching moment.

Chores

Most kids do not like chores. If you feel like a bad parent because you have a hard time getting kids to do chores, take comfort in knowing that kids everywhere consider chores to be a major disruption of their recreation time. But every day, kids need to do something to contribute to the family. Chores are family contributions that always happen to be inconvenient. Some parents even prefer to call chores "family contributions." Every child needs to know that as a member of this family, his or her contributions are needed in order for the household to run smoothly.

As a parent, you know that "work" is a necessary part of a child's healthy development, and household work (or family contributions) trains a child to be responsible, not to mention lightening everyone else's load around the home. When a child grows up and goes off to make a living in a challenging world, the work he learned at home will serve as a foundation to how he performs on the job and in his own home. So, how in the world do you get kids to do chores when they don't want to?

That's what Section 3, Skillfully Correct Children when their Behavior is Displeasing, will show you. But for now, just keep in mind that when you teach children about doing chores, help them feel how important their contribution is to the family, as well as how much you depend on them to help keep the family running smoothly.

Make a list of all the chores that need to be done. A good time to do this is during a family meeting where you can get everyone's input.

I remember when we did this. I gathered the family together and said, "Tonight we are going to make a list of everything that needs to be done to keep our family running smoothly." That produced some eye-rolling and moaning among the children. I continued, "I need your help in identifying everything that needs to be done." We started our list. Most of the suggestions came from me and my wife, but we were open to any input, whether it was positive or negative.

Then we made assignments. It was agreed that Dad would make the money and Mom would do the shopping (spend the money) and be in charge of cooking the meals. We divided up the rest of the tasks among all of us. Doing dishes was unanimously the worst chore. We assigned 2 people on that task. We decided how often the chores would change and came up with a chart. We started on a daily chart that turned into a weekly chart. We bundled chores differently from time to time. The point is, we adjusted the chores according to how we felt would work best at the time, and what the children wanted to try.

Make Your House Kid-Friendly

There are physical changes you can make around the house to help your kids become more responsible, more independent, and feel a sense of empowerment. As your kids learn to take on more responsibility, you will feel less need to micromanage. When trying to get your kids to change a behavior, ask yourself if there are any changes you could make around the house that would help. Here are some suggestions to get you started.

> Post a list of everything that needs to be done when cleaning the bedroom: put dirty clothes in hamper, clean out from under bed, closet floor should be clean except for shoes, vacuum carpet, etc. Invite the child to help make the list and write everything down. The child will be responsible for completing everything on the list.

> Post a list of everything that a child might need to take to school depending on the day. The list would include lunchbox, homework, permission slip, gym clothes, mittens, etc. It would be the child's responsibility to look over the list every morning before leaving for school to make sure nothing is forgotten.

> Designate a shelf, cubby or box for everything that needs to be taken to school. Everything the child needs to take to school

can be put there the night before to eliminate the stress of trying to find everything when being rushed out the door.

Give your child a wristwatch. Then when she is at a friend's house and needs to be home by a certain time, she can easily watch the time.

Put cereal, after-school snacks, and other things that kids need regularly in a place low enough where they can reach.

Provide a lower rod in a closet where kids can get and hang up their clothes without help.

Provide smaller containers for milk, juice and water to allow kids to pour without spilling.

Teach Problem-Solving

Parents often take it upon themselves to solve their children's problems. When they do that they miss an opportunity to teach the skill of problem-solving. I attended a Love and Logic® workshop where one of the sessions was about training children to own and solve their own problems. It got me thinking about how important it is that children learn to solve their small problems while they are young, so they have the know-how to deal with big problems as adults.

Let's say your child comes to you with a problem: "I can't find my coat." "I have no clean clothes!" "I suck at basketball." "Big Brother is teasing me." Here are five simple steps to help you guide your children through the problem-solving process.

Step 1. Acknowledge negative feelings.

Acknowledge negative feelings whenever a child comes to you in distress (see Chapter 6). "Oh no, that's got to make you mad." "Oh man, I'll bet that's frustrating." Or just a simple, "Oh no." Remember, when kids feel heard and understood it frees them to solve their own problems.

Step 2. Hand the problem back.

"What do you think you are going to do?"

Step 3. Get permission to share ideas.

Ask, "Would you like to hear what some other kids have tried?" I love this phrase because it takes the parent out of the equation. Sometimes kids don't like their parent's suggestions because it takes away from their sense of personal power. They don't like to feel that the parent is trying to "control" their decision. But asking if they would like to hear what some other kids have tried gives them a feeling of independence. If that feels awkward or you forget the phrase, say, "Would you like some ideas?"

Step 4. Provide a few ideas.

If the child is interested in hearing some ideas, you have the green light to say:

Some kids decide to ____. How would that work for you?

This is your chance to share your most brilliant ideas. But don't give any hint that you think one idea is better than another. You might inspire your child to come up with some solutions on his own and he might even choose *his* solution over yours.

When you add, "How would that work for you?" to each idea, your child is prompted to consider the consequence of each idea. Don't be afraid to offer a bad idea to get him thinking.

Step 5. Allow the child to choose the solution.

Resist the urge to suggest which solution you think is best. Real learning comes from deciding on a solution, carrying out the solution, and learning from the consequence. End by saying, "If anybody can figure it out, you can. I'd love to hear how it turns out."

Note: If the problem is too big (like, "I'm failing math") or too dangerous (like, "I'm being bullied at school"), then it would be wise for the parent to get involved in the solution.

Here is an opportunity for a mother to teach her son how to solve a problem by giving the problem back to him.

Tommy raced into the house from the back yard. "Joey is calling me names," he cried.

Mom: "Hmmm. That must have hurt your feelings." (Step 1)

Tommy: "It did."

Mom: "What do you think you are going to do?" (Step 2)

Tommy: "What?"

Mom: "What do you think you are going to do?

Tommy: "I dunno. Make him stop."

Mom: "Would you like to hear what some other kids have tried?" (Step 3)

Tommy: "I guess."

Mom: "Some kids decide to call names back. How would that work for you?" (Step 4)

Tommy: "Not good. I tried that."

Mom: "Hmmm. Okay. Some kids decide to just ignore their friend. How would that work for you?"

Tommy: "I dunno."

Mom: "Hmmm. Okay. Some kids decide to play with another friend. How would that work for you?"

Tommy: "I dunno."

Mom: "Well, if anybody can figure it out, you can. I'd love to hear how it turns out." (Step 5)

Can you think of any more options for Tommy to consider? Tommy's decision might be to do nothing. The important thing is that he was empowered to make that decision himself and learn from its consequence.

Let Kids Make Mistakes

Some parents set high standards for their children and when their children fail to meet those standards, they get angry. "No no no. Not that way!" This causes children to feel like a failure, and they will avoid learning new things and stop taking risks for fear of humiliation. They will be sneaky and try to hide mistakes from their parents. Parents who criticize their children for making mistakes take away from their sense of belonging. Criticizing communicates that your love and acceptance is conditional upon them living up to your expectations.

The truth is, kids learn to make good decisions by making bad decisions. A wise parent will allow their children to make poor decisions and experience the consequences while the children are young and the consequences are small and fairly harmless.

Some parents feel if they don't show disapproval or inflict shame or punishment, they are acting permissively and letting their children get away with something. There is a better way. It's not being controlling and it's not being permissive. It's helping children take responsibility for their mistakes and learning from them. Here's what you do.

First of all, realize that kids make mistakes. They just do. Often, when they try something new, they fail. Sometimes they just do stupid things because they do not have the foresight or the knowledge to avoid trouble. Kids gain foresight and knowledge by learning from the poor choices they make.

Second, consider mistakes as opportunities to learn. It is much easier for a child to take responsibility for a mistake if her parents see it as a learning opportunity rather than something bad.

Then you are going to lead your child in the following discussion using the "Three Whats":

1. **What happened?** Do not ask, "What were you thinking?" or "Why did you do that?" Asking "why" gives the child an opportunity to dodge responsibility by putting the blame on something or someone else.

2. **What needs to be made right?** Does anything need to be paid for, replaced, or repaired? Was anyone hurt physically or emotionally who deserves an apology.

3. **What might you do differently next time?** Do not say, "I hope you learned your lesson." Do not tell the child what she should have learned or what she should do next time. However, you can ask: "What might you do differently next time?"

Mistakes are going to happen so expect them and embrace them. Consider mistakes to be wonderful learning opportunities; opportunities to gain insight, knowledge and empowerment. You may occasionally observe your child about to make a mistake and want to jump in and prevent it from happening to protect your child from feeling the pain of failing. If the mistake is not going to be dangerous to anything or anyone, consider allowing the child to make the mistake. A child will learn more from making a mistake than from any lecture or warning from you because natural consequences are the best teachers. Naturally, if you know your child is about to make a dangerous mistake, you need to intervene to prevent it from happening.

If a child decides not to wear her helmet while on a bicycle, then you must step in and prevent that from happening: "Either you wear your helmet, or you don't ride." But if the child decides to ride her bike through a bunch of prickly weeds and gets a flat tire, her experience will be a learning experience she won't forget. The upside for you is, you will get to teach her how to patch a flat tire.

Often, you won't even need to go through the Three Whats: "That's okay, try again," will be all you need to say.

Dad had just purchased a new lawn mower. It was self-propelled, had plenty of power, and even had an electric starter. It was the nicest lawnmower he had ever owned. This was the third time he had used it to mow the lawn and his 12-year-old-daughter, Nicole, asked to take it for a spin. She easily maneuvered it around the front yard and then around the fire hydrant by the curb.

All of a sudden, BANG! The mower suddenly stopped. Upon inspection, it was discovered that Nicole had come too close to the fire hydrant, causing the mower blade to hit one of the bolts coming up from the base of the fire hydrant. Not only had the lawn mower blade been damaged (which was replaceable) but the shaft from the engine to the blade was bent (a major and expensive repair). The lawn mower was inoperable. It had gone from being a shiny lawn mower to a shiny lawn ornament in a split second.

"Dad, I'm so sorry," said Nicole.

Dad was speechless. He knew that whatever came out of his mouth in the next few seconds would be remembered forever by his now trembling daughter. He wanted to tell her how careless she was and how disappointed in her he was for not watching carefully. He wanted to tell her that he expected her to pay for the repairs and if it couldn't be repaired she was going to pay for a new lawn mower and – oh yeah – she was grounded for the rest of the summer.

Instead, he took a deep breath, exhaled and said in a calm voice, "Ok."

Then, he wheeled the lawn mower away. Nothing more was said.

A month later the lawn mower was back from the repair shop, as good as new.

"Let's take it for a spin," Dad said to Nicole.

"No thanks, Dad."

"Nonsense," said Dad, grinning, "when you get bucked off you jump right back on, right? Come on. I trust you."

Nicole reluctantly followed her dad outside. When invited to take the controls, she stayed far, far away from the curb and the fire hydrant.

After the lawn was done, Nicole said to her dad, "Dad, you had every right to lay into me when I broke the lawn mower, but you didn't. Thank you."

Dad just smiled, but inside, he shuttered to realized how close he had come to damaging his relationship with his daughter.

I sure made my share of mistakes as I experimented with new parenting skills. But I didn't give up. Every time I made a mistake I tried to determine what I would do differently next time. And there was always a next time. A home makes a good laboratory for experimenting. You will be an inspiring example to your children when they see you make mistakes.

10

Teach Good Values

Values are guiding principles or personal rules that you choose to follow that influence your behavior and decisions. You live by your values, expecting them to lead you to opportunities and relationships you desire. Values guide you to what you want to become and keep you from getting into trouble.

Guiding values, like belief, hope, and hard work, help you achieve your goals. *Relationship values,* like kindness, honesty and respect, help you connect with people. The Boy Scouts teach a set of values they call the Scout Law: A Scout is Trustworthy, Loyal, Helpful, Friendly, Courteous, Kind, Obedient, Cheerful, Thrifty, Brave, Clean, and Reverent.

You live by values whether you do it consciously or unconsciously. You can identify your values by filling in the blank: It's important to be _____. For example, it's important to be hard working. It's important to be respectful. You try to live by the values you feel are important.

There are also values that might be considered "negative values." They would include, lying, selfishness, arrogance, procrastination, rudeness, disrespect, wastefulness and defiance. Children and adults adopt negative values for reasons that include:

1. They haven't been taught "positive values"
2. They were taught negative values

3. Negative values help them meet their need for personal power

Children learn values as they grow up. They learn values by watching and modeling Mom and Dad. They learn values from watching TV and movies, from their peers, and from social media. If Mom and Dad do not model and teach their children positive values, their children will learn from people who may not have their best interest at heart. *Children who do not live by Mom and Dad's values are destined to live by someone else's.*

For example, here are some values that children might learn from sources outside the family: It's important to have power over women. It's important to get revenge. It's important to feel the rush of watching pornography. It's important to numb emotional pain with drugs, to cheat in school, to receive peer approval by sexting, to drink alcohol, to experiment with marijuana, and to put down other people who are different than they are. Parents need to pass good values on to their children. Here are the three steps to do that:

1. Model the value
2. Teach the value
3. Give recognition when a value is practiced

Model the value. Your kids are watching you. You are their model; their example. They learn by observing. Your example affects your children's behavior more than telling them what to do. If you tell your kids not to smoke, drink, or swear, but you don't model these behaviors yourself, they're more likely to do these things when you're not around. There's an old saying that goes: *Your behavior speaks so loudly that I cannot hear what you say.* If you practice kindness, respect and honesty, your kids are more likely to practice those values too. If you want to pass good values on to your children, you must live by those values, because you can't pass something on that you don't have.

Teach the value. When you model a value, it's easy to teach it. You simply teach what you do. When do you teach? As soon as your children are old enough to understand. Where do you teach? Around the dinner table, at family meetings, while walking the dog together, when driving in the car together, when sitting around the campfire, when tucking kids into bed. Ask questions to get kids thinking:

"Why is it important to be kind?"

"I don't know."

"Well, it makes you feel good and makes the other person feel good too. Do you remember when you helped me look for my keys, and you found them? That made me feel good. How did it make you feel?"

"Good."

"Can you think of other ways you have been kind?"

With older kids and teens, it is harder to teach them values but not impossible. Avoid sarcasm and criticism: "Hey, you might try a little kindness sometime." You can't control another person and make them live by a particular value. But you can have an influence on them by strengthening your relationship with them and modeling the values you want them to adopt. Don't nag or lecture about values. If kids think you are pushing a value on to them, they will resist, maybe even rebel and do the opposite. They have to make up their own minds whether or not to live a value you think is important.

You might start a conversation by asking, "What's a value that you live by?" They might respond, "What do you mean, value?"

Then you can have a conversation about what values are and what values *they* think are important.

Give recognition when a value is practiced. When you give attention to a behavior, that behavior is reinforced and the chance of that behavior being repeated increases. When a child does something good, you can give recognition to the value that is behind the behavior. First, recognize the good behavior. "Wow! You really cleaned the kitchen." Then tack on a value statement: "That was very thoughtful of you. "Thoughtful" is the value. By adding on a value statement, you reinforce the value, which encourages the child to repeat it. Here are some more examples:

Thank you for telling the truth. That shows honesty.

Thank you for rocking the baby to sleep. That was very helpful of you.

I saw you share your toy. That was very unselfish of you.

I noticed that you didn't hit your sister back. That showed a lot of self-control.

I'm going to show you 10 values you can model and teach your children. These are values that *I* think are important and will benefit you and your children. The values that I suggest may not be as important to you as they are to me, and that's okay. Values are a personal thing. I suggest you identify what values are important to you so you can teach them. You are already modeling them.

Keep this in mind as you teach your children values. Your children will be more willing to learn when you have a good connection – a strong relationship with them. So, always be working on strengthening relationships as you model and teach values. Here are 10 values for your consideration:

1. Be kind

2. Be respectful
3. Practice chastity
4. Be educated
5. Be a friend
6. Be trustworthy
7. Take care of your body
8. Never give up
9. Understand the facts about drugs
10 Be spontaneous

1. Be Kind

It's important to be kind.
What if there was a pill that:

>lowered our blood pressure,
>made us feel more energized,
>added years to our lives,
>made us feel happier,
>reduced stress,
>calmed anxiety,
>reduced depression,
>increased self-confidence,
>increased self-esteem,
>AND had no negative side-effects?

What if this pill could help us make a positive difference in other peoples' lives and bring more purpose and meaning into our own lives? What if this pill helped to promote peace within the walls of our home and even within our community? What if this pill was free and readily available?

I imagine you've already figured out that there is no pill like this, but the same benefits can be realized by doing acts of kindness. Kindness changes lives. Both the giver and the receiver benefit.

Kindness is also contagious. People who receive your kindness will be more likely to "pay it forward," creating a domino effect. Even more astounding is that people who only observe you doing a kind deed will be motivated to do a kind deed too. Your kind deed could result in dozens of other kind deeds being done.

Here's the catch. In order for the "kindness pill" to really be effective, it needs to be taken every day. In other words, to receive all the benefits, you must do one or more acts of kindness daily.

How to Teach your Children Kindness

If you want your kids to show kindness, model it. Show acts of kindness yourself and let your children see it or hear about it. They learn by your example. Here are some acts of kindness you can do:

Hold the door open for someone.
Let someone go in front of you in line.
Offer to help someone.
Put a surprise note where your child will find it.
Give someone a compliment.
Volunteer where volunteers are needed.
Say "Good morning" to a person standing next to you in the elevator.
Take a minute to direct someone who is lost, even though you're rushing.
Write a letter to a child who could use some extra attention. Kids love getting mail.

Offer to pick up groceries for an elderly neighbor, especially in bad weather.

Say "I love you," to someone you love.

Help a mother carry her baby stroller up some stairs, or hold a door open for her.

When you're on a crowded train or bus, offer your seat to an elderly, disabled or pregnant person.

Let a fellow driver merge into your lane.

Put your shopping cart back in its place.

Bring a box of doughnuts home to share when no one is expecting it.

Forgive someone a debt, and never bring it up again.

Listen to someone who seems down.

When you start looking for opportunities to perform acts of kindness, they start popping up everywhere.

When you show kindness to someone, they feel that they matter.

Teach your children about doing acts of kindness, and then do them together. Together you will share the benefits described above, plus:

1. You will cheer someone up, you will certainly surprise them, and you might change someone's life for the better.

2. You will both feel good – the kind of good you cannot feel any other way.

3. When you extend acts of kindness into to the universe, good things will find their way back to you.

4. By doing acts of kindness with someone else, you strengthen your relationship with that person.

Anytime you do something to help someone or to cheer them up, you are doing an act of kindness. Here are a few suggestions of things you can do with your child.

Within Your Family
- Do a family member's chore
- Bring the groceries in from the car
- Make a picture for someone
- Make someone breakfast in bed
- Give someone a manicure
- Style someone's hair
- Leave a kind note for someone
- Wash the car
- Make or buy a treat and share it
- Teach a skill you have become good at
- Make someone's bed
- Help a younger sibling with homework
- Call or write to a grandparent
- Do the dishes even when it's not your turn
- Volunteer to change the baby's diaper
- Invite someone to play a board game with you
- Make someone popcorn while they're watching a movie

Within Your Neighborhood
- Mow someone's lawn
- Rake someone's leaves
- Shovel snow off someone's driveway or walks
- Brush the snow off someone's car
- Bake cookies or a cake for someone
- Weed someone's flowerbed
- Walk the neighbor's dog
- Clean up dog poop

Babysit for free

For Anyone
Pay for a stranger's lunch or dinner at a restaurant
Donate time to a local charity
Return a shopping cart
Send a handmade card to someone
Send a care package to someone living away from home
Offer your seat to someone
Write a letter to someone thanking them for something they did
Buy your friend some ice cream
Help someone move in or out
Assist someone who looks like they could use some help
When everyone else is gossiping about someone, be the one who says something kind
Give someone flowers
Let someone in the grocery store with only one or two items go ahead of you
Put sticky notes with positive slogans on the mirrors in restrooms
Hold the elevator for someone
Help someone who is struggling with carrying something

To get the most benefit from doing acts of kindness, expect nothing in return. One way to add to the fun is to do an act of kindness anonymously. One exception to this is when you give someone food. People like to know where the food came from, so include a note or deliver it to them in person.

Use appropriate caution when it comes to doing acts of kindness for people you don't know. Do not let your child approach strangers alone.

2. Be Respectful

It's important to be respectful.

To show respect to our children, we can let go of old disrespectful methods of parenting like spanking, punishing, screaming, threatening, and treating children as though they had no rights or deserved no explanations. We can refrain from saying, "Because I said so" as a reason for setting an expectation. Instead, we use a calm voice and use words like, "please", "thank you", and "excuse me." We work on strengthening our relationship and explain, *why,* when we set a new expectation. We ask for their advice or input on things, and listen to their opinions. We *show* them how we would like them to treat us.

To show respect to our spouse we can do kind things for them, apologize when necessary, compliment them, listen to them, seek their opinion, never criticize, come to their defense when necessary, never complain about them behind their back, and spend quality time with them.

One of the best things you can do for your children is to show respect to your spouse. When kids see Mom and Dad doing kind things for each other, helping each other with household responsibilities, talking kindly to each other, disagreeing and working out differences, hugging and spending quality time together, it makes them feel safe. It shows boys how to treat women, and shows girls what to look for in a man.

If you are a single parent, you cannot model respect with a spouse. You can, however, *teach* respect; teach boys how to treat women and teach girls what to look for in a man.

Parents who treat each other with *disrespect*, who argue, criticize, show no affection, or go so far as to cause physical pain, can expect their children to feel anxiety and fear. That leads to all the negative behaviors we don't want our children to exhibit. These kinds of parents would do well to seek help to build a better relationship, not only for themselves, but for their posterity.

There are two kinds of respect, respect for ourselves, and respect for others. To show respect for ourselves (or show self-respect) we can treat ourselves with care: exercise, eat healthy food, avoid things that will harm us like smoking, drinking alcohol, pornography, drugs, too much screen time and too much time playing video games. We will avoid putting ourselves down by saying things like, "I am so stupid" or "I'm such an idiot." We will avoid saying sarcastic things to ourselves like, "Nice job, Dummy." Instead, we will encourage ourselves with, "I can do better than that," "I can't quit now," and "I won't let this setback keep me down." We won't curse or use profanity because such language gives children a license to do the same. Kids learn from how we treat ourselves and will treat themselves the same way.

Family meetings provide a good opportunity to talk about respect. Here is an example of how a family meeting with small children might go.

Start by asking, "What is respect?" If you get a bunch of blank stares, you might ask, "Is respect saying 'Please' and 'Thank you?'" (You're looking for a, "Yes.") "Is respect apologizing when you've hurt someone's feelings?" "Yes, that's right." "Does respect mean to always agree with someone?" "No. You can be respectful and not agree." "Does respect mean to be kind?" "That's right, it does." "Does respect mean to tease?" "No, that's right. Instead of teasing, what can we do?" "Be kind. That's right." "Can we say that respect means acting nice and talking nice?" "How does it make you feel when someone treats you with respect?" "Good. Yes. Me too." "How do you think others feel when you treat them with respect?" "Yes, they probably feel good too." "When you treat people with respect, do you think they will feel more like treating YOU with respect?" "What are some other things we can do to show respect?"

Continue your discussion until you have come up with a short list of actions that show respect. Write the list on a white board or piece of paper. Better yet, have one of the children do the writing. Your list might include:

Say "Excuse me," when you bump into someone
Say, "I'm sorry," when you hurt or offend someone
Ask before borrowing
Knock before entering
Say, "Please," and "Thank you."
Say, "Nice to meet you."
Talk nicely
No screaming, threatening, hitting, making fun of, or calling names
Do kind things
Clean up your mess
Keep promises
Do what Mom and Dad ask
Be polite
Wash your hands before you eat
Don't interrupt

Keep it simple and easy to remember. Children should also understand what it means to be disrespectful. Ask them what it means to be disrespectful:

When you bump into someone and don't say, "Excuse me."
When you hurt or offend someone and don't say, "I'm sorry."
Borrowing without asking

Entering without knocking

Forgetting to say, "Please," and "Thank you."

Forgetting to say, "Nice to meet you."

Talking mean

Screaming, threatening, hitting, making fun of, or calling names

Doing unkind things

Not cleaning up your mess

Breaking promises

Not doing what Mom and Dad ask

Being impolite

Not washing your hands before you eat

Interrupting

End the discussion with a challenge to practice being respectful to everyone, especially family members, over the next week. Then plan on getting together at the end of the week and talk about how things went; what went well and what didn't. During the week, try to catch your children in the act of being respectful and acknowledge them: "I noticed that you said, 'Thank you.' That showed respect."

Let your children know that you expect them to be respectful to Mom and Dad and to their siblings. If you have been working to strengthen your relationships with your children, your kids should be willing to try. Don't expect them to be perfect. When children are in distress, mad, embarrassed or frustrated, they are more likely to be disrespectful. When that happens, do not focus on their disrespect. Instead, acknowledge their negative feelings (See Chapter 6).

Have your family come up with a code-word(s) that everyone can use to remind someone that they just did something or said something that was disrespectful. For example, the code-words might be, "Let's start over." Then, when a child answers in a disrespectful way or fails to say, "Please," or "Thank you," you can say, "Let's start over." Then repeat the situation, allowing the child to do it right.

If you catch *yourself* saying or doing something disrespectful in front of your children, like screaming, you can say, "Let's start over," then repeat the situation in a respectful way. This is a positive way to correct disrespectful words or actions and be a good model for your kids. Be consistent with not allowing disrespect within your family.

3. Practice Chastity

It's important to practice chastity.

Simply put, chastity means not engaging in sexual activities until marriage. What is meant by sexual activities? Anything that leads to sexual intercourse, including passionate kissing and touching sexually sensitive parts of the body.

Sexual intercourse results in young people becoming parents before they are ready, which can lead to abortion, giving up a child to adoption, or grandparents unexpectedly becoming new parents again.

Disregarding chastity can turn a young person's life upside down, both emotionally and financially. It can result in guilt and shame and leave emotional scars. And I haven't even begun to name the disadvantages a child faces after being born to a child who is not ready to be a parent. It's just not worth a few moments of carnal pleasure.

Kids say, "Don't worry. I can stop anytime. I won't let it go any further than kissing. I know what I'm doing." That statement will not hold up. Here's what happens when two kids engage in passionate kissing. Their brains create a chemical cocktail that gives a natural high. This cocktail is made up of three chemicals, all designed to make us feel good and crave more: dopamine, oxytocin, and serotonin. These three chemicals combine to light up the pleasure centers of the brain. Dopamine can stimulate the same area of the brain activated by heroin and cocaine, resulting in a feeling of euphoria. Oxytocin, otherwise known as the "love hormone," gives a feeling of affection and attachment. Serotonin gives a feeling of belonging and significance. If kids do not feel a sense of belonging and personal power at home, passionate kissing can help meet those needs.

These three chemicals combine during passionate kissing to cause your children to let their defenses down and give them a craving to engage in touching and feeling, and ultimately, intercourse. So when kids say, "Don't worry I can stop anytime. I won't let it go any further than kissing. I know what I'm doing," they can be sincere and committed at the time, but when they are in the middle of kissing passionately, their self-control gets overridden by their cravings for more – just like an addiction, and their resolve to control themselves can go out the window.

As new grandparents you become long-term babysitters. That's because most young teens are not mature enough to take on the responsibility of parenthood. Instead of night-time feedings and regular diaper changes, they want to be running track and hanging out with friends. Instead of dealing with colic or ear infections, they want be going to dances and designing their futures.

Kids will say, "I'll use birth control," or "I'll get an abortion." Regarding birth control, it doesn't always work. And abortion –

does your daughter want to carry around the thought for the rest of her life that she ended someone's life? Does your son want the emotional weight of permitting his child to be destroyed?

Here are a few more reasons why chastity is a good idea.

Sleeping around puts one at risk for contracting various Sexually Transmitted Diseases (STDs). STDs are infections that are passed from one person to another through sexual contact. The causes of STDs are bacteria, parasites, yeast, and viruses. There are more than 20 types of STDs, including Chlamydia, Genital herpes, Gonorrhea, HIV/AIDS, Syphilis and Trichomoniasis. If a pregnant woman has an STD, it can cause serious health problems for the baby. Even if kids use condoms, which they don't always do, there is still a risk of catching or spreading STDs. The most reliable way to avoid infection is to not have vaginal, oral or anal sex.

How does premarital sex affect marriages? Studies have shown that men and women who have engaged in casual sex before marrying each other are at greater risk for divorce. Even people who have sex with each other before they get married have a higher risk of an unhappy marriage.

Unwed teenage mothers have a high probability of long-term poverty and welfare dependence – something they normally don't think about during a make-out session.

Those who disregard the value of chastity run the risk of experiencing depression, feeling guilt, and even considering suicide. Some girls feel that in order to keep their boyfriend, they must have sex with him. This is a myth, and anyone who has had sex for that reason will tell you so. Even with all that has been said, there is still another reason to practice chastity. Chastity is a commandment from God.

If you believe in a higher power or in deity or in a God, then there are probably some guidelines or commandments concerning chastity. I believe in God. He is our Heavenly Father. We are his children. He wants us to be happy. What father wouldn't? So, he gave us commandments and told us that if we follow them, it will guarantee our happiness. He also told us if we disobey his commandments, it will bring us unhappiness. He will never force us to obey His commandments. We all have the freedom to choose whether or not to obey.

Our Heavenly Father gave us the gift of feeling amazing, beautiful emotions during a passionate kiss, touch, and intercourse. But He warned us that these emotions should only be felt and shared with the person to whom we are married. The Apostle Paul said that it is *"the will of God"* that we *"abstain from fornication,"* which is sexual intercourse between an unmarried person and anyone else (1 Thessalonians 4:3).

Our Father also wants us to return to Him and inherit Eternal Life. That means an eternity of happiness with our Heavenly Father and all of our earthly family. The Apostle Paul said, *"Know ye not that the unrighteous shall not inherit the kingdom of God?"* Then he went on to list those who would not be eligible. The list includes *fornicators* and *adulterers* (1 Cor. 6:9).

Moms. Dads. Teach your children about the value of chastity. Teach your sons to treat girls with respect, not as objects used to satisfy lustful and selfish desires. Teach your children that until they are married, they must avoid passionate kissing, lying on top of another person, and touching the private parts of another person's body, with or without clothing. In other words, don't do anything that arouses sexual feelings. Teach your children to avoid movies, TV shows or even discussions with friends that would arouse sexual feelings. Teach them to avoid pornography like the plague.

As a parent, it's important to set a good example for your children. If you avoid TV, movies, and discussions that arouse sexual feelings, the greater the chance your kids will too.

Teach your children that sex is a wonderful, beautiful way to show your love for that one person with which you want to spend the rest of your life – within the bounds of marriage. Teach them before they start to learn from their peers. Don't leave the task of teaching the value of chastity to schools, churches, or other organizations. No one can teach this important value in as warm and loving ways as you can. No one has the relationship you have with your kids.

Dress Modestly

Teach your children to dress modestly. Modesty is a value closely related to chastity. Let's face it, when boys see a girl dressed immodestly, their sexual urges ignite. Your daughter's clothes send out an unspoken invitation for men to treat her the way she looks. An immodest outfit will attract boys to her *body*. They will treat her as an object, not as a person.

However, when a girl dresses modestly, she is inviting boys to realize that she has more to offer than just her body. Modesty shows that she has dignity and is looking for a guy who treats her with respect and wants to get to know her as a person. The way girls dress influence everything from the people they meet to the way they dance to the conversations they have.

Immodest clothing is any clothing that is revealing in any manner. Young women should avoid short shorts, short skirts, shirts that do not cover the stomach, and clothing that does not cover the shoulders or is low-cut in the front or the back. Young men should also maintain modesty in their appearance.

Some parents feel embarrassed to speak frankly to their children about sexual intimacy. If you start early, around the age of 8 years old, it's easier than after they grow older. That's right, 8 years old.

Our society speaks quite freely about casual sex and gives parents very little support in teaching and honoring moral values like chastity. TV and movies make a mockery of chastity and personal virtue. They glorify one night stands without any concern for the risks people take when they participate in casual sex. Children who do not have the benefit of learning about chastity from their parents will develop their attitudes about it from friends, television, movies and social media.

4. Be Educated

It's important to be educated.

Do I really have to convince you how important it is to be educated? I doubt it, but here are some advantages of being educated that you can pass on to your children. The more educated you are:

the better career options you have.
the more you can help others.
the better your ability to turn your dreams into reality.
the more confidence you'll have.
the less likely you will be exploited and fooled.
the less likely you will become poor and homeless.
the greater your ability will be to make more money.
the more enhanced your life will become.

Homework

Some kids view homework as a nuisance because it hinders sports, social, and extracurricular activities. Always consider homework a top priority. If your child cannot complete all homework, and do it well, then you need to set an expectation: "As long as your homework gets completed to my satisfaction, you can keep attending your sports, social, and extracurricular activities. Otherwise, you'll have to cut back somewhere. Your homework comes first." And then follow through if you need to.

Grades are important, but...

Grades are important. They're the standard measurement of how well children are doing in school. High school grades matter most if your child has hopes of going to college. Colleges put a lot of weight on grades when deciding who will be admitted.

As important as grades are, they are not as important as the learning. An employer cares more about the knowledge and skills an employee brings to his business than what his grades were. If your child was going to start her own business, grades would not even be an issue. What would matter is the knowledge and skills your child brings to the business. It's the knowledge and skills acquired in school that will make a difference in the child's future. Teach your children to study to get good grades, but more importantly, study to learn. Make love of learning a priority.

5. Be a Friend

It's important to be a friend.

Here are some things you can teach your children about being a friend.

Everyone needs true friends. They will influence your decisions, your thoughts and your actions. There is a saying that goes, "Show me your friends and I'll show you who you are." Good friends share values and help each other be a better person. However, if any of your friends urge you to do something that is wrong, stand up for what is right, even if you stand alone. You will feel good about your decision and others will be influenced by your example.

Appreciate differences. Make an effort to be a friend to those who are shy or lonely, have special needs, or do not feel included. Getting to know who they really are might surprise you. To have good friends, be a good friend. Here are some tips to being a good friend:

Be trustworthy. If you say it, do it.

Tell the truth even when the outcome will not be in your favor.

When you make a mistake, admit it.

When friends make mistakes, forgive them.

Keep secrets.

Always be there for them.

Don't judge or criticize.

Listen. Just listen.

Share. Be unselfish.

Be loyal. Tell them, "I've got your back." If you hear people criticizing your friend, stand up for that friend.

Be vulnerable. Let your friend see who you really are by sharing your fears, shortcomings and weaknesses.

If you see your friend about to make a poor choice, express your feelings.

6. Be Trustworthy

It's important to be trustworthy.

Being trustworthy means that you are worthy of someone's trust; that you are dependable and reliable. It means that if you say you are going to do something, people can count on you to do it, even if you don't say, "I promise." Being trustworthy also implies:

1. You are honest – even when the outcome will not be in your favor.
2. When you make a mistake, you admit it.
3. You will make every effort to be on time.
4. You can keep a secret.
5. You will defend your friends even when they are not present.
6. You will apologize when necessary.

Do you recognize that being trustworthy and being a friend are closely related?

Teach your children that being trustworthy means choosing not to lie, steal, or deceive in any way, and that being trustworthy leads to peace of mind and self-respect. Teach your children to be honest at school and not to cheat in any way.

Be the kind of parent your children can trust with sensitive issues without being criticized or humiliated. Show them that they can approach you without fear of being yelled at, lectured or punished if they admit to a lie or confess a wrong-doing.

7. Take Care of Your Body

It's important to take care of your body.

This is another value where your example is so important. When children see you taking care of your body, the chances they will do the same will increase. Please consider the following ways to model proper care of your body.

Do not smoke.
Do not drink alcohol.
Do not misuse drugs.
Do get enough sleep.
Do drink lots of water.
Do exercise.
Do eat healthy food and avoid eating too much unhealthy food.
Do brush your teeth.
Do wash your hands.

Then in a family meeting, or in the car, or around the dinner table, you can discuss the importance of taking care of your body, and what you can expect if you don't take care of your body.

8. Never Give Up

It's important to never give up.

Once again, this is a value you can model.

Look at the people around you. *Everyone* who you would consider a success has encountered failures, setbacks and defeats. Everyone else has also encountered failures, setbacks and defeats but they settled for less. What's the difference? Winners always get up after they fall. They dust themselves off, learn from their failures and keep trying. They never give up.

As I was writing this book, I hit many roadblocks. Life's demands kept coming at me making it hard to find time to write. I experienced "writer's block." I had doubts this book would be accepted because I'm not an eloquent writer. I knew my book would be competing with hundreds of other parenting books. My "limiting beliefs" were sometimes overwhelming. There were times when I thought of giving up. But I focused on "why" I wanted to see my dream materialize. I wanted to make a difference in parents' lives. In my mind I could see parents reading my book. I could see them experimenting with new ideas and watching their children's behavior change. I could see relationships being strengthened, and kids learning good values from their parents. I had a vision of parents raising good kids with the help of my book.

I had a theory and I still do, that if enough parents read and apply the advice in my book, the number of good kids would increase. And as the number of good kids increased, the amount of crime, gun violence, drug abuse, sexual abuse and all of our other social problems would decrease. My "why" gave me the motivation to persevere. I did not give up. And now look. You are reading my book.

So here is some advice that I gleaned from successful people that you can teach your children. Don't hang with people who have given up on their dreams and would discourage you from achieving your dreams. Winners believe in themselves when no one else does. When the tough moments come, when people say you can't do it, when the elements combine to beat you down, do not quit. Do not give in. Do not settle. Make your "why" powerful. Focus on it. In those tough moments, as you persevere, you develop character to fight harder. And as long as you keep fighting you will eventually achieve your goal. And when you achieve your goal, you acquire more self-confidence to go after your next goal.

Teach your children that it's okay to fail. No one likes to fail, but failing is a necessary part of learning. Sometimes people talk themselves out of trying because they are afraid of making a mistake. Don't be afraid to make a mistake. Every time you make a mistake you learn. And every time you learn, you get smarter about how to achieve your goal. Expect mistakes. Embrace mistakes.

Some of the most famous people and companies started from humble beginnings.

In their first year of business, Coca-Cola only sold 400 Cokes.

Michael Jordan was cut from his high school basketball team.

Dr. Suess' first children's book, *And to Think that I Saw It on Mulberry Street*, was rejected by 27 publishers. Vanguard Press, the 28th publisher, sold 6 million copies of the book.

The book, *Chicken Soup for the Soul* was turned down by 33 publishers before Health Communications agreed to publish it. Since then, over 7 million copies of *Chicken Soup for the Soul, A 2nd Helping of Chicken Soup for the Soul*, and the *Chicken Soup for the Soul Cookbook* have been sold worldwide, with the books translated into 20 languages.

If Michael Jordan, Dr. Suess, Coca-Cola, and the authors of Chicken Soup for the Soul had given up, they wouldn't be the household names they are today. These inspirational stories serve as living proof that if at first you don't succeed, you must try and try again.[1]

There are countless other people who you will never hear about who have successfully achieved their dreams because they never gave up. I want you to believe that you and your children can be among them.

9. Understand the Facts about Drugs

It's important to understand the facts about drugs.

You may ask, "Is this a value?" I propose it is. You can't be with your children all the time to protect them from harm. The next best thing is to arm them with knowledge so they can make wise decisions and take good care of themselves. So when it comes to drugs, kids need to hear the facts from you. Teaching about drugs is beyond the scope of this book, but there are a few important things every parent should know.

If you use drugs, you model that behavior for your children. More specifically, if you smoke, drink, or use drugs in any way not prescribed by your doctor, you set the example for your kids to follow.

Many parents are unaware of how much their children are exposed to drugs every day. Kids hear about drugs from friends, TV, music, social media, the internet, and from people dealing drugs. There is a high probability your children know how to get drugs. If they are 13 years old or older, there is a good chance they have been offered drugs. Go ahead, ask them. If they haven't been offered drugs yet, you can assume they will be someday. Do your children know what to say and do when that happens? Teach your children the facts about drugs and what to do if someone tries to get them to experiment.

There is a short online government publication that offers a wealth of information about drugs. It is called *Growing up Drug Free – A Parent's Guide to Prevention.*

https://www.dea.gov/sites/default/files/2018-06/growing-up-drug-free-2017.pdf

This would be a good place to begin your fact finding. It helps parents find answers to questions like:

1. What drugs do kids use?
2. Why do kids start using drugs?
3. How do I talk to my child about drugs?
4. What if my child is using drugs?

10. Be Spontaneous

It's important to be spontaneous.

Doing something spontaneously can give you an emotional boost and put some fun into you day. If you do something spontaneous with you children, they will receive the same benefit.

One day I was working at the computer when I heard the front door open and my daughter yell, "Anybody home?"

I always love it when my children come to visit.

"Is Mom here?"

"Come on in," I said.

"I can't stay long," she said, "I just need to talk with Mom for a minute."

I looked out the front window because sometimes she brings one of her children along. There was her daughter, my 11-year old granddaughter, sitting in the passenger seat of the car. I thought I'd go talk with her. I opened the car door and sat down behind the wheel.

"Hi, Grandpa," she said.

We talked for a minute, and then I said, "Hey, what are you doing right now?"

She said, "Just talkin' with you."

I said, "Do you want to go for a ride?"

135

Her eyes got big and she said, "Sure, I guess."

I started the car and we backed out of the driveway. My daughter and my wife leaned out the front door and I could read my daughter's lips as she said, "Where are they going?"

I loved the puzzled look on her face. We waved goodbye, and my granddaughter and I rode around for about 10 minutes and had a wonder conversation. We rolled back into the driveway about the time my daughter was ready to go.

Our ride together gave us a bit of a thrill and boosted our moods because it was unexpected and a bit daring. It was fun and no doubt added an experience to our lives that we could look back on and smile.

The idea here is to do something out of the ordinary.

Try a new recipe

Try a new restaurant

Go into a store you have never shopped in and try something on that you would never wear

Call an old friend just to say hello

When your kids are least expecting it, announce that you're all going out for ice cream. Or, gather your family together to eat ice cream out of the carton

Turn up the music and dance with your kids

Learn a magic trick

Have a pillow fight

Train for, and enter a 5 or 10K race

Start a journal

Get a new hair style

Instead of eating lunch, go for a walk

Pray

Invite another family (or lonely person) to join your family for dinner

You can use this value to do something out of the ordinary regarding the nine values described above:

1. Be kind. If you see an opportunity to help someone, don't hesitate, take it.

2. Be respectful. Go out of your way to ask someone for their opinion or to give them a compliment.

3. Practice chastity. If someone shows you pornography on their electronic device, take it and throw it in the garbage.

4. Be educated. Take a class and learn something brand new, like yoga.

5. Be a friend. Approach someone you've seen around the office or school and introduce yourself.

6. Be trustworthy. When confronted with the options of doing the popular thing and doing the right thing, choose the right thing.

7. Take care of your body. If you pass by a gym, stop and ask for a tour.

8. Never give up. Make failure, embarrassment and self-doubt your motivation to pick yourself up and try again.

9. Understand the facts about drugs. Drop into a drug recovery center and ask for a brochure on drug addiction and whether or not they need volunteers.

10. Be spontaneous. Do something that you otherwise would never consider if you weren't looking for something spontaneous to do.

A Few Bonus Values to Consider

There are many more values to consider. I just want to run a few of them by you.

Be accepting: Respect others regardless of skin color or cultural differences.

Be compassionate: When you see someone in need, do something about it.

Be courageous: Do what you know is right regardless of other's opinions.

Be generous: Give something you have, including your time, to make someone else's life better – sometimes requiring sacrifice.

Be peaceful: Resolve conflicts without using force or violence.

Be positive: Look for something good in all situations.

Be responsible: Make sure important things get done, and if they don't, don't pass the blame onto something or someone else.

Have integrity: Stick to your values even when no one is watching.

Show self-control: Be able to choose your response in tough situations instead of reacting to them without thinking.

Be polite: Use good manners and act in socially acceptable ways. Use these phrases when appropriate:

Please
Thank you
May I
Excuse me
No, thank you.

Sometimes values conflict. For example, a neighbor brings your family a plate of cookies. Upon tasting them, you all agree they are the worst cookies you've ever tasted. A few days later, your neighbor is visiting and asks how you liked the cookies. If you say they were good, you'd be lying. If you say they were terrible, you might be considered unkind. What are you going to do? That might be a good question to discuss at a family meeting. Let me know what you decide.

11

Teach Desirable Behavior

One of the biggest frustrations parents have is the daily struggle to get their children to obey rules and expectations; to do what they're told. The struggle occurs because parents care that their children are safe, clean, kind, helpful, and cooperative. But kids put exploring, having fun and feeling good at a higher priority. It seems the more parents try to get their children to cooperate, the more children resist. But kids need rules and boundaries. And they need to clearly understand what is expected of them before cooperation can happen.

The purpose of this chapter is to teach that rules must be understood before they can be enforced. Some rules don't need a lot of explaining, and some do. When a child breaks a rule, then you will use techniques to enforce the rule, which will be covered in Section 3. But before you can enforce the rule, you must, of course, set the expectation or make the rule, and the child must understand it.

There are three ways to make rules. As you move from one to the next, you will notice more emphasis is placed on helping your child understand the rule. Use the one you feel is best depending on the age of your child and the difficulty of understanding the rule.

1. Quick and easy

2. Get the child to repeat the rule
3. Teach a skill

Quick and Easy

"Hey, no jumping on the couch!" is a quick and easy way of making a rule. Most rules are made on an as-needed basis, right? You don't know a rule is necessary until you see a need for it. "Take your muddy shoes off at the door." "Ride your bike on the sidewalk, not in the street." "Eat your cookies in the kitchen, not in the living room." "Dirty clothes go in the laundry basket."

Rules made the quick and easy way, however, may not make a very big impression. Children can tune you out when you give them, conveniently forget them, consider them a one-time deal, or regard them as unimportant. They might even test those rules later to see if their parents are serious about enforcing them. That's their job. Kids are good at dodging or finding loopholes in rules made the quick and easy way.

Get the Child to Repeat the Rule

You do this by 1) getting the child's attention, 2) explaining the rule, and 3) having the child repeat the rule back to you. This will increase the chance that the child will understand and remember the new rule.

"Hey, no jumping on the couch! Come here. Couches are for sitting. Not for jumping. So, I'm going to make a rule, no jumping on the couch. Can you remember that?" The answer will always be "yes." Kids can be pretty good at tuning you out and telling you what you want to hear. Then you'll say, "Okay, what's the rule?" They'll say, "umm, I forgot." You'll remind them, "The rule is, no jumping on the couch. So, what is the rule?" When they repeat the rule to your satisfaction, then you compliment: "That is exactly right. Thank you."

Will you have to remind them again? Probably. "Hey." you say in your calm voice. "I see you jumping on the couch" In many cases, this is all you will need to say in order for them to remember the rule. No lecture is necessary. But if they appear to have forgotten, simply say, "What's the rule?" Don't let them ignore you. Repeat if needed, "What's the rule?" They will look down and shrug their shoulders. "The rule is no jumping on the couch. What is the rule?" When they repeat the rule to your satisfaction, then you are done. "Good. That is exactly right." The child's self-esteem remains intact. Later, and this is important, give attention to good behavior: "I noticed you haven't jumped on the couch for a long time." Then give a fist-bump.

Teach a Skill

Some rules take a little more training; training that would resemble teaching life-skills from Chapter 9. Watch how Mom teaches this next rule:

"From now on I would like you to wash your hands by yourself when I call you for dinner. I'm going to show you what I expect, okay? Come with me. First, put the stool in front of the sink. Very good. Now get on the stool and turn the hot and cold water on so it's warm. Go ahead and try. A little hotter. Great. Now get your hands wet. Good. Now, one squirt of soap. I want you to scrub your hands all over. Keep scrubbing and count to 10. Slow down. Now rinse. Make sure all the soap is rinsed off. Nice job. What do you think you do now? That's right. Turn off the water. Now what? Dry them. Are we done? Not quite. One more thing to do. What is it? (pointing to the stool) That's right. Put the stool back where it goes. You got it. So what are you going to do when I call you for dinner? That's right, wash your hands. Do you know why I want you to wash your hands before dinner? Because dirty hands can make you sick. So, why do we wash our hands before dinner? That's exactly right."

To a parent, clean hands mean: all the dirt goes down the drain. To a child, clean hands could mean: get my hands wet and wipe the dirt off on the towel. You cannot assume a child knows what clean hands mean without *teaching* what clean hands mean.

You'll notice that Mom never said, "Do you understand?" A child will always respond "yes" to that question whether he understands or not. Mom had her child actually do everything she wanted her child to understand and remember. She had the child go through the motions of washing his hands which teaches so much more than simply explaining. She also explained *why* this expectation was set: because dirty hands can make you sick. She kept it very simple.

Now Mom needs to enforce the rule. She will watch from a distance to see if her child follows her expectations. If the child forgets to wash, Mom will calmly remind him by saying what she sees: "I see hands that are not washed."

If the child makes a good effort but does not do a good job at washing, Mom will let it go in the beginning. She will not expect perfection. She will expect mistakes. This is not the time to criticize. What is important is that Mom looks for good behavior, no matter how small, and rewards it: "I noticed you went into the bathroom to wash your hands when I called you to come to dinner. Thank you." She wants the child to feel good about whatever he did right. If more training is necessary, she will do it sometime before the next meal. "Hey. Let's practice washing our hands. Come with me."

Don't forget, when a new expectation is set, always give attention to the new, good behavior. Your positive feedback reinforces the behavior (more on this in Chapter 13)."

I used to say, "Let me *smell* your hands." If they smelled like soap, I'd acknowledge their good behavior.

Teaching a skill requires more time than the other two methods. Some parents say they don't have the time. I suggest you can either spend time teaching, or spend time dealing with the same misbehavior over and over again.

Even a household responsibility as simple as putting toys away deserves proper training. Don't say, "When I say, 'Time to clean up,' then you clean up. Do you understand?" That's not clear enough. Say something like, "When I ask you to clean up, you need to stand up right away, pick up a toy, put it in the toy box. Pick up another toy, put it in the toy box. And keep doing that until all the toys are picked up." Then demonstrate by putting toys in the toy box yourself. After that, invite him to try it: "Let's practice. I'll ask you to clean up and you show me what you need to do. Tommy, would you please clean up?" Do the practice. This way Tommy understands by doing. And you can approve the way he does it or correct the way he does it by asking questions: "Is that a toy I see over there in the corner?" Make sure Tommy understands what the room should look like when the job is done: no toys on the floor – all toys in the toy box. "There, now nobody will step on any toys." Make sure the last thing you do is approve the way he does it. "You got it Tommy. That's exactly what I want you to do."

Some skills may require more time to learn. For instance, loading a dishwasher may require you and your child to load the dishwasher together for two or three days. You will teach which dishes go on the top rack and which dishes go on the bottom – and why, how to position the dishes on the racks, how to tell if a dish requires rinsing before loading, how to position the silverware and smaller items, what kind of soap to use, and how to start the dishwasher after it is loaded. Instead of criticizing, ask questions. "Is there any way to fit these last two dishes in there?"

Then you will invite your child to do it by himself, at which time you will exhibit superhuman patience and withhold criticism, because your child will do something different to make it his own unique way. It's a personal power thing. As long as the dishes are getting clean, don't sweat the details.

Did you notice in the previous two examples after the child was invited to try it, I advised against correcting the child with statements like, "You missed a toy over there," or "Move these bowls closer together to make room for a couple more dishes?" I suggested using a question instead: "Is that a toy I see over there in the corner?" "Is there any way to fit these last two dishes in there?" Questions encourage kids to think; to solve problems, which will help them learn and remember.

If you want to keep your children's attention and help them understand something important, ask questions. Questions also soften criticism, and when a child is learning something new, criticism is discouraging.

Over time, your young apprentice will develop her own unique method for doing whatever it is you trained her to do. Don't criticize or correct just because it's not your way. If the job is getting done, it's all good. She is simply finding a positive sense of personal power by doing it her way.

Please consider the following when it comes to teaching desirable behavior:

1. A good relationship is the foundation of effective teaching. Kids will be more receptive to your teaching if they have a good relationship with you. They will want to please you and they will feel bad if they disappoint you. To put it another way, if you don't have a good relationship with your children, they will treat your teaching as if it were a lecture and then go off and behave as though you never had the conversation. When you have a rocky relationship with your children, teaching is difficult, and for the most part, ineffective.

2. All children have a need for limits and boundaries. This need is wired into every child. Clear, enforced limits and boundaries make children feel safe, secure, and assured their parents care about them. Limits and boundaries are necessary to provide a sense of order in the household, keep kids safe, and teach respect for each other.

3. Tell them why. You shouldn't have to explain the reason for every rule. The first two ways to make rules (1: quick and easy, and 2: get the child to repeat the rule) as explained above, do not explain the "why." However, if your child understands that there are simple reasons for your rules, he'll be more likely to comply. It also shows respect for your children and when you respect your children, they are more likely to respect you. So when you set an expectation, decide if it's prudent to explain why.

4. Let children help make the rules. Explain the situation and invite the children to create a rule. You might start the conversation by saying, "When we go out to eat as a family, what rules do you think we should all follow?"

5. Rules teach self-discipline. Limits and boundaries actually teach kids to set limits for themselves. When children *choose* to obey a rule, particularly one they don't want to obey, they learn to delay immediate gratification, which strengthens their self-discipline.

6. Expect kids to break rules. That's what they do. They test limits and boundaries. Sometimes they will break a rule just to see what you will do. If children continue to break a rule, then it's time to problem-solve together (Chapter 20) or add a consequence to the rule (Chapter 21).

The Problem with "Don't"

I want you to think about all the times when you teach your child desirable behavior by telling him what *not* to do. "Don't jump on the couch." "Don't leave your dirty clothes on the floor." "Don't wander off." "Don't walk in the puddle." "Don't write on the wall." "*Don't*" does not teach a child what he is supposed to do instead. So when you use "don't," try to follow it up with what you prefer he do instead: "Don't walk in that puddle! Walk around puddles." "Don't leave your dirty clothes on the floor. Dirty clothes belong in the hamper." "Don't jump on the couch. Couches are for sitting." "Don't wander off. Stay next to me." "Don't write on the wall. Write only on paper."

Sometimes, when you tell your child to not do something, it gives him ideas on how to get your attention. When you say, "Don't tease your sister," in his subconscious mind he might be thinking, "Thanks for the idea, Mom."

You can't encourage cooperation or correct misbehavior unless you have set clear expectations. So if you're having a hard time getting kids to obey the rules, it might be that the children don't clearly understand. Teaching desirable behavior can lead to better understanding and cooperation.

12

Model Good Behavior

Your children are always watching what you do. They observe how you treat other people. They watch how you handle stress. They see how you practice what you teach. Being a positive role model is one of the most effective things you can do to influence your children. Don't want your kids to smoke, drink, do drugs, swear, or watch pornography? Being a non-smoker and refraining from drinking, doing drugs, swearing, and watching pornography will go a long way in shaping your children's desire to do the same.

Want your kids to be kind? Let them see you hold the door open for someone, let someone go in front of you in line, or offer help to someone. Want your kids to be respectful? Let them see you say, "Excuse me," when you bump into someone, say, "I'm sorry," when you hurt or offend someone, or ask before you borrow something.

Want your kids to always tell the truth? Model being honest even when telling the truth would not be in your favor.

Want your kids to learn better skills for resolving conflicts? Let them see you resolving conflicts with your spouse, your friend, or your neighbor.

Your children will imitate what they see you do. Here are a few examples of teaching your children *negative* values by what you do.

A father spends much of his time playing computer games, but tells his 13-year-old daughter she spends too much time playing computer games. She learns that playing computer games is okay as long as dad doesn't notice.

A mother tells the cashier at a movie theatre that her 12-year-old son is only 11 so he can get in at a discount. Her son learns it's okay to lie.

Parents teach their daughter to treat everyone with respect yet they often neglect to say "Please," and "Thank you." Her daughter learns that if she doesn't practice respect, it's okay.

A mom and dad argue frequently, sometimes yelling, criticizing, and saying sarcastic things. The children learn to treat each other the same way when they are upset.

A father tells his children not to swear, but swears profusely when someone cuts him off in traffic. The children learn that it's okay to swear so long as someone makes them mad.

A mom tells her son to stop putting his fingers in his mouth, but when she's nervous, she bites her fingernails. Her son learns that it's okay to put his fingers in his mouth no matter what his mom says.

A mother tells her daughter to be kind to others, yet allows the bus driver to pull out when she sees someone running for the bus. Her daughter learns you don't have to be kind if it's not convenient or in your best interest.

While smoking a cigarette, a father tells his son he should never start smoking. The son has already decided that whatever is good enough for Dad, is good enough for him.

I guess you have to ask yourself the question: are you the kind of person you want your children to imitate? If not, then you can expect some challenging behavior.

13

Give Attention to Good Behavior

Giving attention to good behavior is one of the most effect ways to improve behavior. It reinforces good behavior and makes children want to cooperate. Please read the following statement carefully because it is the foundation of this principle; the reason it works.

The behavior that receives the most attention is the behavior that will happen the most.

Will you agree with me, that most of the time, the behavior that receives the most attention is the bad behavior? Well, if the above statement is true, and I'm claiming it is, then the following statement must also be true.

If you pay more attention to good behavior, good behavior will happen more often.

Experts in child behavior say this is one of the best ways to replace misbehavior with cooperation. I've seen it work and I know parents who were amazed at how quickly their children's behavior changed when they applied this principle. Here is what you do:

Look for good behavior and give it attention.

Giving attention to good behavior means watching each of the children, and when one of them behaves in a good way, rewarding him or her with positive attention. Here are some examples:

I noticed you were nice to your sister all morning.
I noticed you came when I called the 1st time.
I noticed you did the dishes without being asked.
I like it when you chew gum with your mouth shut.
I'm impressed with how nice your room looks.
Thank you for cleaning up your spill.

Acknowledge children when they are in a good mood, playing together nicely, doing what you asked, not causing trouble, and generally behaving well. This makes children want to behave well because whatever behavior receives the most attention is the behavior that will happen the most.

Your children need your attention. Attention meets their need for a sense of belonging. When you give attention for desirable behavior, that behavior is reinforced. The attention feels good, so they do the same thing again, expecting to receive more of your attention. And if they get your attention again, they make a connection: doing that behavior gets me attention. I think I'll continue to do that behavior. If you give good behavior more attention, good behavior will happen more often.

Here is the challenge. Usually when children are behaving well, it's easy to ignore them. "Leave well enough alone," you might say. Don't ignore children's good behavior. Watch for opportunities to give attention to good behavior.

Even children who are *always* misbehaving will accidently do something right. You might say, "I noticed you walked past your brother without teasing him. Thank you."

The more positive attention you give a child who exhibits good behavior, the more you will reinforce that behavior. You have to watch for opportunities. Sometimes you have to watch really hard.

Imagine a child who gets many rewards a day. The positive attention feels good. It is meeting his need to belong. He wants more. He's being noticed. He feels accepted by receiving your attention without having to misbehave to get it. Why misbehave to get attention when it feels good to behave? Children who are not used to being rewarded for good behavior will thrive on the shower of rewards you give them. They will behave well because they like receiving your unsolicited attention and approval.

Dr. Glenn I. Latham, in his book, *The Power of Positive Parenting*[1], states: "Research has shown that the most effective way to reduce problem behavior in children is to strengthen desirable behavior through positive reinforcement rather than trying to weaken undesirable behavior using aversive or negative processes." Dr. Latham feels this statement is so important, he includes it at the end of every chapter.

For children who misbehave often, give attention to good behavior as often as you can. For children who misbehave less often, you might think it unnecessary to give so much attention to good behavior, but keep this in mind: If your good-behaving children see you giving more attention to your misbehaving children than they are getting, they might draw the conclusion that to get more of your attention, they should misbehave more. To keep that from happening, distribute rewards evenly and sincerely among all of your children. Kids from toddlers to teens will thrive on your positive attention.

If you are watching more than one child, you have your work cut out for you. But the result will be worth it and you will be glad you made the effort.

If giving attention to good behavior seems overwhelming, just do the best you can. After a while it will seem so natural that you will do it without even thinking about it.

You can also give attention to good behavior later, upon hearing about it. Dad might come home from work and say, "Mom said you put on your shoes the first time you were asked. Nice going."

Don't make a big deal out of giving positive attention. Just two or three seconds is all it takes. Don't let too much time go by without catching each child doing something right, and rewarding each child with kind words or actions. Below is a list of ideas to say or do to get you started. Use them liberally when you see the opportunity.

Positive things to say:

Good thinking.

You're really using your head.

Good idea.

You did it!

Nice going. Gimme five.

Well done.

I couldn't have done it better myself.

I couldn't have done it without you.

You and I, we make a good team.

I had no idea you colored so well.

You're getting better at staying inside the lines.

I didn't know you could read so well.

This is good work.

You guys are playing together so nicely.

Hey, that's pretty good.

You're getting better.

That's neat.
You make it look easy.
Thank you.
You didn't quit.
I really appreciate you helping.
You should be proud of yourself.
I see you've decided to share your toys.
You are helping your sister draw.
This looks great. You must have worked hard at it.
That was a really good try.
I love listening to you play the piano.

Anything that starts with "I notice..."
I notice you are sitting quietly.
I noticed you were nice to your sister all morning.
I've noticed that you've really been in control.

Anything that starts with "I like…"
I like the way you are sharing.
I like how you did that.
I like that idea.
I like the colors you chose.
I like it when you chew with your mouth shut.
I like how you did that the first time I asked.

Anything that starts with "I'm impressed…"
I'm impressed with how nice your room looks.
I'm impressed that you didn't hit your sister back.
I'm impressed with how you took care of the baby.

Anything that begins with "Thank you…"
Thank you for doing that without an argument.
Thanks for doing what I asked.
Thank you for doing that without being asked.

Positive things to do:
>a hug
>a pat on the back
>a high-five
>a low-five
>a touch on the shoulder
>a soft punch on the arm
>a fist bump
>a smile
>a thumbs-up
>a note left for them to find
>a card they receive in the mail from you
>a laugh (with them, not at them)
>a wink
>a wave
>a touch on the arm

Paul Axtell, in his book, *Ten Powerful Things to Say to Your Kids*[2], says, "Your words have the power to create. What are you creating for your child with your words? If you see something in your child and you acknowledge it, that characteristic will continue to develop and grow. Whether it's positive or negative, whatever you pay attention to grows. So choose the good things to focus on."

When you give attention to good behavior, make sure your rewards are sincere, evenly given to all the children, and done frequently. When you use this skill, your children will show good behavior more often and unwanted behavior less often.

Another way to give attention to good behavior is to write a note: "I noticed you shared your crayons with your brother this morning. That made me smile." Slip the note in his lunchbox, coat pocket, inside his book cover; anywhere he will find it.

Try a little experiment

Choose one negative behavior you'd like to see your child change. Decide what the opposite behavior would be. For example, the opposite of not getting into bed when asked is getting into bed when asked. The opposite of teasing your little brother is not teasing your little brother. Then watch for a small glimmer of the opposite (positive) behavior. When you see it, give it attention. "You got ready for bed much faster tonight. I like that. Thank you." Or, "I noticed you played nicely with your bother for 10 minutes. High five."

14

Offer Choices

Making decisions gives kids a sense of personal power. Let's take another look at what it means to have a need for a sense of personal power. Personal power means to feel in control of one's self or the situation. It means having the freedom to choose. Kids want to feel empowered and significant. They don't like feeling controlled by someone else.

Children who do not have a strong relationship with parents do not like their parents telling them what to do, so they rebel. They feel they can take back their personal power by 1) saying "no" to requests, 2) disregarding rules, and 3) doing the opposite of what parents ask. This usually results in a power struggle:

"You'll do it because I said so."
"No I won't."
"Yes you will."
"No I won't."

When parents get into a power struggle, they never win.

However, giving kids choices gives them a sense of personal power, and when a child has a couple of options to consider, putting up a struggle might not even cross her mind.

Give your kids a choice whenever you would normally choose something for them. Instead of giving them a breakfast cereal, offer them a choice: "Would you like this cereal or this cereal?" Or ask for their opinion: "Which soap should I put by the sink, the bar soap or the squirt soap?" Offer two options, each of which you like. Here are some more examples:

Do you want potato chips or corn chips in your lunch?

Do you want the green towel or the blue towel?

Do you want juice or milk?

Which outfit do you want to wear, this one or this one?

Shall we read this book or this book?

Do you want to brush your teeth first or shall I brush your teeth first?

Do you want to go to the park before or after lunch?

Shall we have sloppy-joes or grilled cheese sandwiches?

Shall we go to the post office or the bank first?

Offering choices is a simple but powerful way to give kids daily doses of personal power. You can also use choices to get kids to do something they don't want to do:

Do you want to load the dishwasher or clean up dog poop?

Would you like to clean the living room or the bathroom?

Do you want to do your homework at the table or up to the counter?

Do you want to brush your teeth in the bathroom or the kitchen?

Would you like to go home now or in 10 minutes?

A father in one of my parenting classes told this story. He went home after class and was telling his wife how we had talked about giving children choices. It was time for the kids to get ready for bed. He had a daughter who didn't like getting ready for bed. He leaned over to his wife and said, "Watch this." He called his daughter by name and said, "It's time to get ready for bed. Do you want to take a bath or a shower?" She yelled back, "Shower." He said, "Okay," and without any argument or stalling, she headed off for the shower. He said his wife's jaw dropped. She couldn't believe what just happened.

This is a simple skill but very powerful. I was teaching a preschool teacher who had a student that didn't like to take orders. She said it was time for the children to stop playing on the rug and sit up to the table. Her stubborn student ignored her request. Then she called him by name and said, "Do you want to sit in the red chair or the blue chair?" "Red chair," he said, got up, came over to the table and sat in the red chair.

One more. My daughter and her family were visiting me and my wife. They had to leave in five minutes. My son-in-law made an announcement: "We need to go. Do you want to leave now or in five minutes?" "Five minutes," was the consensus. "Ok, I'm setting my alarm," he said. When the alarm went off, everyone got up and headed for the car without a bit of complaining.

If your child cannot make up her mind, you can say, "If you don't choose, then I will choose for you." If your child chooses something that was not one of the choices, you can make the choice for her.

Parent: "Do you want milk or water?"
Child: "soda pop."
Parent: "Water it is."

When do you use choices? Regularly throughout the day, whenever you would normally choose something for your kids. Instead of choosing for them, let them choose.

Section 3

Skillfully Correct Children when their Behavior is Displeasing

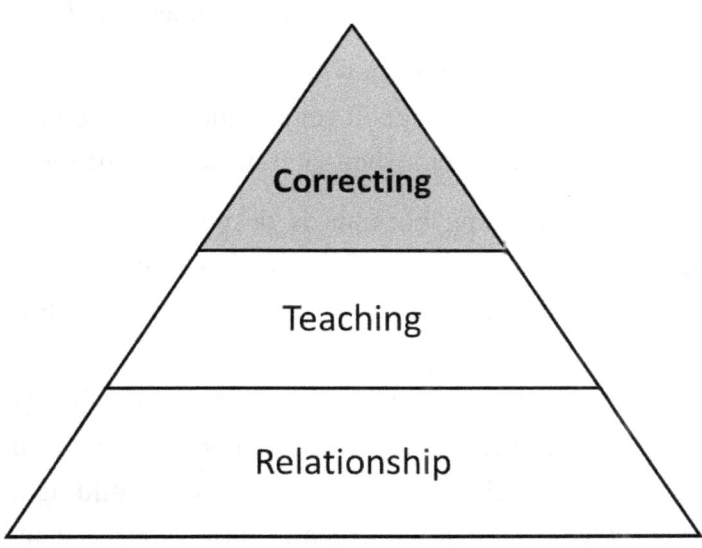

Up to now, we have talked about what you can do to *prevent* misbehavior from happening. Now we are going to look at some things you can do *when* your children misbehave; when they test boundaries and choose not to obey the rules. This is where typical parents focus their attention. They skip relationship building and teaching, and focus on correcting misbehavior. Then they wonder why their children don't listen and why they seem so rebellious.

Parents should not have to spend most of their time correcting their children, and they won't have to if they follow The 3-Step Parenting Formula.

As a reminder, The 3-Step Parenting Formula goes like this:

1. Build a strong relationship with your children
2. Teach them life skills, good values, and desirable behavior
3. Skillfully correct them when their behavior is displeasing

The 3-Step Parenting Formula is designed to show you that teaching is the foundation of correcting, and strengthening relationships with your children is the foundation of both teaching and correcting.

If you have trouble getting your child to do what you ask, instead of intensifying your efforts to correct your child, you should focus on teaching your child. If your child ignores or disregards what you teach them, turn your attention to strengthening your relationship. A good relationship is the key to effective teaching, and effective teaching is the key to effective correcting.

This section assumes that you have or are working on strengthening relationships with your children, and that you have spent time teaching them the desirable behavior that you expect. This section will show you how to skillfully correct your children when their behavior is displeasing. But first, let's take a look at what *not* to do. Following are nine practices that some parents use that undermine all the good they accomplished when they worked to strengthen relationships and teach desirable behavior.

15

Nine Practices that Undermine Progress

There are some things that parents do to correct their children's misbehavior that do not work and should be avoided. These are common practices that will weaken relationships and cause children to be disinterested in anything a parent tries to teach them.

1. Screaming
2. Spanking
3. Punishing
4. Lecturing
5. Criticizing
6. Bribing
7. Threatening
8. Counting to three
9. Timeouts

Let's take a minute to examine why these practices don't accomplish our desire to improve behavior in the long run. They might improve behavior for a short time, but parents who use these practices, find that misbehavior returns again and again, making them a waste of time and effort.

1. Screaming

Screaming at your kids makes them feel devalued; the same you would feel if someone screamed at you. Instead, practice using your calm voice and you will notice a sense of calm settle over your entire household.

2. Spanking

Opponents to spanking say spanking produces shame, fear, and humiliation, which can lead to a child thinking, "I'm a terrible child. I deserve abuse. I'm unworthy of being loved." Their self-esteem takes a nose dive. They do poorly in school and can become depressed.

They say once you start hitting you are at risk of losing control.

They say spanking teaches kids not to get caught. It does not teach kids to obey a rule because it's the right thing to do. For example, when a child is spanked because he lied, the message he receives is, *don't lie or you'll get spanked*, rather than, *don't lie because lying hurts others and that's wrong*.

Spanking teaches kids not to get caught, but when no one is watching, they feel they can get away with anything.

3. Punishing

Punishments, in the form of threatening, spanking, grounding, timeouts, and removing privileges may be able to control a child's misbehavior temporarily, but do not address the root cause, so the misbehavior is bound to happen again and again and again. Misbehavior is the way children say, "Hey, I have unmet needs over here."

L. R. Knost, in her book, *Two Thousand Kisses a Day*[1], says, "While the temporary 'payoff' of punishment may be compliance, the need behind the behavior is never addressed and those needs merely get driven unground and often emerge later in more potentially damaging behaviors such as lying, sneaking, anger, outright rebellion, depression, aggression, addictions, etc."

Misbehavior is the symptom of an unmet need, as discussed in Chapter 2. When we address the symptoms with punishment, the problem doesn't go away, it intensifies. Punishment separates children from their source of guidance and comfort just when they need it the most. Not only do parents miss a golden opportunity to teach their children how to cope with their distress, but they hurt the very relationship that kids need to feel safe in expressing their emotions.

Jane Nelsen, Ed.D., in her book *Positive Discipline*[2], says, "Where did we ever get the crazy idea that in order to make children do better, first we have to make them feel worse? Think of the last time you felt humiliated or were treated unfairly. Did you feel like cooperating or doing better?"

4. Lecturing

Children do not respond well to lecturing. I know that parents want to share their wisdom in hopes that their children will see the error of their ways and never make the same mistake again. Parents think that the longer their lecture, the more it will sink in. I get it. I used to be that parent. I've learned since that when parents go on and on, kids tune them out. Lecturing is a waste of time and effort for parents. It also gives children the feeling that parents do not think they are capable of understanding without a long sermon. Here's a rule of thumb. The less said, the more impact it has.

5. Criticizing

The first principle Dale Carnegie teaches in his timeless book, *How To Win Friends & Influence People*[3], is to stop using criticism as a means to change people. Although he is speaking about people in general, it applies to parents. He writes, "Criticism is futile because it puts a person on the defensive and usually makes him strive to justify himself. Criticism is dangerous, because it wounds a person's precious pride, hurts his sense of importance, and arouses resentment."

Whenever I hear a successful athlete being interviewed, he or she will give the reason for achieving great success by saying something like, "The coach always gave me encouragement and that motivated me to be the best I could." You will *never* hear an athlete say, "The coach criticized me all the time and that motivated me to do the best I could."

Think of the last time you were criticized. Did it motivate you to strive to do better, or did it hurt your feelings. Did is cause you to want to improve, or did it cause resentment. Children are no different. Criticism does not motivate children to improve their behavior. It does not create a desire to cooperate. Criticism contributes to misbehavior.

6. Bribing

Bribery is offering a reward in the middle of misbehavior. "Ok, stop crying and I'll buy you that candy bar." "Ok, if you mow the lawn, I'll give you 10 bucks." The problem with bribing is that it trains kids to expect a reward for misbehaving. They misbehave; they get offered a reward to cooperate. They will figure out that anytime they want a reward (and that would be consistently throughout the day) all they have to do is throw a tantrum or refuse to do what you ask.

7. Threatening

A threat is something you tell your kids but never follow through on. "If you don't clean this room up right now, you can forget your sleep-over this weekend." Your threat is empty and your kids know it. Avoid making statements like: "You promise you'll never do it again?" and "Ok, but this is the last time." A threat like, "You'd better do what I told you or you'll be sorry," may, in fact, sound like a challenge to a stubborn child. You will soon learn about following through and letting consequences do the teaching.

8. Counting to three

Counting to three is a little like threatening. It's like saying, "You'd better do what I told you by the time I get to 'three' or you'll be sorry." I've seen counting to three work. I've used it. But parents have to come up with something to make the child "sorry" if they get to three, like a timeout or a punishment of some sort. Also, when you count to three, you condition your children to listen to you only when you count.

9. Timeouts

Time-out is a favorite tactic parents use to 1) stop the behavior, and 2) teach a child that that kind of behavior will not be tolerated. There are two problems with time-outs:

1. Time-outs invite power struggles. When a strong-willed child is directed to stay on the time-out chair or ordered to his

bedroom, it becomes the parent's job to make sure he stays put for the duration of the time-out, while the child's job is to try to escape. Each attempt to escape adds fuel to the fire, turning a 5-minute time-out into a 30-minute ordeal leaving both parties frustrated and both parent and child forgetting the reason for the time-out in the first place.

2. Even a compliant child who is willing to stay put during the duration of the time-out will most likely learn nothing from it. After all, do you really suppose a child in time-out is thinking about what they've done and how they plan to change their ways? A time-out is nothing more than a punishment and seldom teaches a child the important lesson he needs to learn. More effective ways to teach is through problem-solving or letting consequences do the teaching, which you will learn about in this section.

What is common to all nine of these practices?

1. They are usually done in the heat of anger.

2. Most parents do them because they don't know what else to do.

3. They work. They are a quick fix to getting kids to cooperate, but the fix is only temporary.

4. They create a disconnection between parent and child. They undermine the progress a parent has made to strengthen the relationship they have with their child.

5. These practices are about the parent, not the child. Parents hate the feeling that their kids are "winning." Parents turn to using these practices when their own power feels threatened and they feel the need to get back their power.

6. They should never be used.

You may be thinking, "If these nine practices should never be used, then what *should* I do instead?" The remainder of Section 3 will give you the skills to effectively correct your children. Experiment with them and see if they don't make a good replacement for these 9 practices that undermine progress.

16

Start with These Skills

There are various reasons kids choose to test limits and boundaries. Sometimes they forget, sometimes they just don't want to obey the rule. Sometimes they test you to see what you will do; to see if you will be consistent in enforcing the rules.

It's essential to **be consistent in enforcing the rules**. Enforcing a rule one day and letting it go the next can cause kids to test the rule continually. Then, when you want to enforce the rule, it's hard to get the children to follow it. If children think they can get away with ignoring one rule, there's a good chance they will try to get away with ignoring other rules. They will come to believe that you don't mean what you say. The bottom line is this: *when you make a rule, the children should expect you to enforce it.*

Keep in mind that kids cannot obey a rule if there is no rule to obey. Chapter 11 shows how to teach desirable behavior and set rules. The following skills will help you guide your children back to staying within the limits and boundaries you have set.

Describe What You See

Here is a simple way to enforce a rule: describe what you see.

Rachelle is eating food where food is forbidden.

Describe what you see: "Rachelle, I see you eating food over the carpet."

Todd is playing when he should be doing his homework.
Describe what you see: "Todd, I see you not doing homework."

Jennifer leaves her coat on the floor.
Describe what you see: "Jennifer, I see your coat on the floor."

Mike does not put his dirty dishes in the dishwasher.
Describe what you see: "Mike, I see your dirty dishes still on the table."

No need for threats, commands, or lectures. Short, simple statements, and the child's self-esteem is left intact. Your short observations cause children to think, *"You see my dirty dishes? Oh yeah, I'm supposed to put them in the dishwasher."* This technique also requires little time and effort on behalf of the parent.

Use One Word

Here is another short and simple way to enforce a rule. It requires very little effort but works like a charm. Kids also appreciate it because they don't get lectured. And sometimes less is more. The less you say, the better it works.

Rachelle is eating food where food is forbidden.
Use one word: "Rachelle. Food."

Todd is playing when he should be doing his homework.
Use one word: "Todd. Homework."

Jennifer leaves her coat on the floor.

Use one word: "Jennifer. Coat."

Mike does not put his dirty dishes in the dishwasher.
Use one word: "Mike, dishes."

Express How You Feel

When children break rules and you can feel yourself starting to get angry, you can express yourself in a respectful, but assertive manner without attacking or blaming the other person. Attacking or blaming puts others on the defense and is not an effective way to change someone's behavior.

It is common for a parent to say something like, "You always leave your bike in the driveway," or, "You never put tools away after you use them," or, "You make me mad when you wear my clothes without asking." Beginning a statement with "You…" as in "you always," "you never," or, "you make me," causes children to become defensive and blame someone or something else for their behavior rather than take responsibility for their actions.

A better way to express yourself respectfully and assertively is to use phrases that begin with the pronoun "I." In other words, focus on how the behavior makes *you* feel.

Dr. Haim Ginott, in his book, *Between Parent and Child* [1], says, "In troublesome situations, parents are more effective when they state their own feelings and thoughts without attacking their child's personality and dignity. By starting with the pronoun 'I,' parents can express their angry feelings and describe their child's disapproving behavior without being insulting or demeaning."

Keep the focus on:

1. How you feel
2. When you feel that way

3. <u>What</u> can be done to make things better

Here are some examples:

"Rachelle. (1) I get real angry (2) when you eat over the carpet. (3) Food belongs in the kitchen!"

"Todd. (1) It makes me mad (2) when I see you playing when you are supposed to be doing your homework. (3) When your homework is done, then you can play."

"Jennifer. I don't like it when I see your coat on the floor. Coats belong in the closet."

"Mike. I get so upset when you do not put your dirty dishes in the dishwasher because it makes more work for me. When all your dirty dishes are in the dishwasher, then you may leave the kitchen."

"When I see you hit your sister, I get angry. I can never allow you to hurt her."

You can use the last three skills in combination, and with increased intensity if needed:

Describe what you see: "Rachelle, I see you eating food over the carpet." Rachelle does not appear to be listening.

Use one word: "Rachelle, Food." Still, no response.

Express how you feel: "Rachelle. I get angry when you eat over the carpet. Food belongs in the kitchen! And it makes me just as mad when you ignore me. Now go."

Use "I Feel" Statements

"I Feel" Statements are a variation of expressing yourself when you are upset. Every statement starts with "I feel..." There are four parts to an "I Feel" statement. They are the same as above with number 3 being added as an option:

1. "I feel ____" (state how you feel)

2. "When you ____" (when you feel that way)

3. "Because ____" (explain why their behavior causes you to feel this way - optional)

4. "I want ____" (what can be done in the future to make things better. End with an agreement: "Can you do that?")

Instead of saying, "You always leave your bike in the driveway," you would say, "I feel upset when you leave your bike in the driveway because I have to get out of the car to move it. I'm also afraid I might not see it one day and run over it. I want you to make sure your bike is on the lawn or somewhere else before I get home from work. Can you do that?"

Instead of saying, "You never put my tools back when you're done using them," you would say, "I feel mad when you don't put my tools back after you use them because I have to go looking when I need them. I would really appreciate it if you would put tools away when you are done using them. Okay?"

Instead of saying, "You make me mad when you wear my clothes without asking," you would say, "I feel mad and disrespected when you wear my clothes without asking. Would you please ask before you take them?" Notice that step 3, the "because..." step was left out. It's not always necessary if the reason is obvious.

When you put the emphasis on what *you* are feeling, rather than on the child, you can express everything you need to say without accusing, criticizing or attacking. Here are three more examples:

"I feel angry when you leave your dishes in the sink instead of putting them in the dishwasher because I shouldn't have to clean up after you. I need you to put your dishes in the dishwasher. Do you think you can do that?"

"Every afternoon I pick you up after school. I don't mind doing that. In fact, I enjoy seeing you. But I feel frustrated when I have to wait a long time for you to come to the car. So what I want you to do is to be out to the car by 3:15. Can you do that for me?

"I feel unappreciated when I take you places and you forget to tell me 'thank you.' I need to hear a thank you. Will you please thank people when they do something for you?"

As always, be on the lookout for good behavior so you can give it attention. When your child shows up to the car on time or thanks you for the ride, acknowledge it: "Thank you for being on time." Or, "Thank you for thanking me for the ride."

Stop, Redirect, Reward

Sometimes a child will become angry and hit or kick another child. Sometimes an angry child will try to break something. For example, seven-year-old Mason is angrily hitting his younger brother David.

First, **STOP** the behavior. Calmly and immediately stop the hitting by taking Mason gently by the arm and moving him a safe distance from his brother David.

Look him squarely in the eye and say calmly but firmly, "You are really mad." It's important that you acknowledge his negative feelings. It's those feelings that caused him to be angry. If you address only his behavior and not take into consideration his feelings, you will only be addressing the symptoms of a deeper problem. Continue to acknowledge his negative feelings as described in Chapter 6. Then, let him know that it's okay to be mad, but it's not okay to hit.

Second, **REDIRECT** the behavior. Redirect the boy's behavior by giving him a choice: "Would you like to play with your cars or help me in the kitchen?" It isn't enough to simply stop the behavior. The behavior must be stopped and then redirected to a better behavior. This is important for two reasons: First, it gets the child doing something other than hitting his brother. Second, it gets him doing something worthy of some positive attention.

Sometimes redirecting a child means going along with him and doing something together, like a putting together a puzzle or kicking the ball. Otherwise he could fight the redirection and refuse to move. When you go with him, you help him get past his anger and let him know that he doesn't have to face his bad feelings alone. If you don't have time to play at the moment, let him hang with you for a while.

Third, **REWARD** the child for good behavior. After the child has been behaving properly for a few minutes, you have the opportunity to give attention to good behavior. "You've been playing with your toys very nicely. Thank you." Then you gently touch his arm.

Give Advance Warning

If the child is in the middle of doing something she enjoys, and you are going to require that she stop and do something else, give some advance warning in the form of a choice: "Susan, we need to go. Do you want to leave now or in five minutes?" She'll say in five minutes. Then say, "Okay, I'll set my alarm for five minutes." When the alarm goes off, the alarm is the bad guy, not you.

Giving advance warning in this way helps you meet the child's need for a sense of personal power while at the same time, prepares her to do something she doesn't want to do.

Cooling-Off Period

Sometimes one of your children will do something that really sends you over the edge, causing your blood to boil and steam to come out your ears. When emotions run high, you tend to say hurtful things, make rash decisions, and impose extreme punishments even when you know better. It's a natural reaction.

In situations like this, it is better to put some distance between you and your child and allow some time to calm down and think rationally. Ask your child to go to his room. "Son, I'm so mad right now I need to take some time to calm down. We will talk about this in a few minutes."

There is no need to feel that you must address the misbehavior immediately. It is better to postpone communication between the two of you for a while rather than run the risk of saying something that you will regret later. So go to that happy place in your mind and hang out there while you regroup. Then, when your blood pressure has returned to normal and you can think clearly, come together with your child to work on solving the problem.

Below is a recap of points discussed above. Turn to these ideas when tense situations call for immediate help:

Describe what you see
Use one word
Express how you feel
Use "I feel" statements
Stop, Redirect, Reward
Give Advance Warning
Cooling Off Period

17

Ignore Annoying Behavior

Many of the things your kids do that drive you crazy should not be given any attention at all. In chapter 13 – Give Attention to Good Behavior, we learned an important principle: the behavior that receives the most attention is the behavior that will happen the most. If that is true, then the following must also be true:

The behavior that does not get any attention is the behavior that will go away.

If you pay attention to annoying behavior, it will likely continue. If you ignore annoying behavior, it will likely stop. When kids argue and tease one another, just walk out of the room. Much of the time they are simply performing for an audience: you! And if you pay attention to them, it encourages their performance.

When kids are showing annoying behavior, it's a normal reaction for you to want to scream, "Stop that right now!" Resist the urge. Instead, pretend it's not happening. Remember that annoying behaviors are usually just normal, growing-up behaviors. Some kids do annoying things just to see if they can get a reaction out of the parent. Don't get caught in their trap. Pay no attention to annoying behavior, don't look at it, comment about it, roll your eyes or shake your head. Leave the room if you must.

Now, with that said, you have to decide whether the behavior should be ignored or not. Behaviors that should be ignored are those behaviors that bug us, annoy us, and frustrate us. They can be whining, pleading, teasing, complaining, arguing, even throwing a tantrum. As long as no one is getting hurt (physically or emotionally) and no property is in danger of being damaged, feel free to ignore. As simple as this sounds, it is difficult for most parents to do because it runs contrary to how we normally respond to such occurrences.

You ask your child to vacuum the carpet. "Why should I have to vacuum all the time?" he complains. "There are other people here. They make just as much mess as I do. Why don't they have to vacuum? I'm sick and tired of always being asked to do stuff. I've got a life too, you know."

If you want to escalate the anger and encourage arguing, jump into the argument. "It will take you all of 10 minutes to vacuum. Why don't we change jobs? I'll do what you do and you do what I do? Think that would make you happier? I know it would me!" As much as you are tempted to respond with something that feels so logical and rational, don't respond. Don't shake your head, roll your eyes, or show any reaction. Then when he or she is done ranting, you can say, "I'm not going to argue about it." Once the chore is done, give attention to good behavior: "That sure looks better. Thank you." You'll get a response like, "Whatever," which you will ignore. Behaviors that get no attention are behaviors that dry up and blow away.

You say to your child, "I'd like you to be home by nine o'clock." You might get this: "Nine o'clock?! Why so early? Can't I stay 'till ten? Even nine thirty? I'm not a baby, you know. Why do you treat me like a baby?" to which you listen with no reaction, and then respond with, "That's exactly right. Nine o'clock. Thank you." No arguing, no fighting, no lecturing.

Give an Ignore Warning

You may want to try warning your child that the next time he does something worthy of ignoring, you are going to ignore him. That way the child will know what you are doing. For example, when you are not on the phone, you could say, "Sit down here, I have something to tell you. You know how when I'm on the phone sometimes and you have a question and can't wait for me to finish my phone call? Well, from now on, I want you to wait. If you try to ask me a question while I'm on the phone, I'm just going to ignore you. It's not that I don't love you or that I don't care, I do. And I'll be glad to help you after I'm done with my phone call. So, just so I know you understand, when I'm on the phone, what do I want you to do? That's right wait until I get off the phone. And what will I do if you want to talk with me while I'm on the phone? That's exactly right. I will ignore you."

Let's say that you have a child who throws tantrums. While your child is calm, you could say, "Honey, I want to tell you something. You know how sometimes when you want something and I tell you 'No', and you feel mad and scream and cry and kick your legs? Well, from now on, when you do that, I'm going to ignore you. That means I will pretend that you are not there. It's not that I don't care, I do. And I'll be glad to talk with you after you're feeling better. So, next time you get mad and scream and cry and kick your legs, what am I going to do? That's right. I will ignore you. But I will still love you."

Now this is important. If you noticed your child waiting for your phone call to end, or you notice an abnormally short tantrum, be sure to reward the good behavior. "I noticed you waited for me to get done with my phone call. Okay, what did you need?" Or, "I noticed that you controlled yourself better. Do you want to talk?"

Here is a quick review:

1. If you pay attention to a good behavior, it will happen more often. (this is a good thing)
2. If you pay attention to an annoying behavior, *it* will happen more often. (this is a bad thing)
3. If you ignore an annoying behavior, it will go away. (this is a good thing)
4. If you ignore a good behavior, *it* will go away. (this is a bad thing)

18

When-Then Statements

In her book, *If I Have to Tell You One More Time*[1], Amy McCready describes a technique she calls "When-Then." This technique minimizes back-talk, whining, and complaining. The main concept behind When-Then is to delay or deny a normally occurring privilege until the undesirable task has been completed.

See if this scenario sounds familiar. You ask your daughter to do something. She says, "It's not my turn," or, "I did it yesterday." Or she ignores you altogether. You find yourself reminding or logically arguing why she has to do it. Then you think you could do it easier and quicker yourself, but you are tired of doing what you asked her to do, so you resort to what has worked in the past. You yell. You don't want to but it seems to be the only thing that works. She finally starts to do what you asked her to do. Now you feel guilty for yelling and wonder if there is a better way. This technique could be the better way.

The skill works like this: WHEN you're done doing what I want you to do, THEN you can do what you want to do. No longer will you have to listen to, "Do I have to?" or "It's not fair!" It shuts down any chance of an argument. Here's how it works:

Ben: "I'm going over to Jack's."
Mom: "Are your chores done?"
Ben: "I'll do them as soon as I get back. I promise."

Mom: "**When** your chores are done, and done to my satisfaction, **then** you can go over to Jack's."

Ben: " But mom…"

Mom: [Calmly walks away.]

Mom walked away so Ben had no one to argue with. He now has a choice. He can do his chores and go to Jack's or not do his chores and not go to Jack's. Here are the guidelines to using When-Then statements:

1. Develop the "When." This is the task you want your child to complete: empty the dishwasher, clean up dog poop.

2. Develop the "Then." Think of a normally occurring privilege that your child *wants* to do that must be postponed until the task has been completed. It should be something close to the time the task needs be completed. "When your hands are washed, then you may have a cookie." Getting the cookie is the obvious privilege in this case.

3. Say your When-Then statement in a calm voice. When you first start using this technique, emphasize the words WHEN and THEN. "WHEN you finish folding your clothes and putting them away, THEN you can use the computer." After you've used this technique for a while your children will come to understand that when you start a request with "when," you mean what you say and there's no point in arguing.

4. You may have to inform the child that this is not up for debate: "This is not up for debate," or, "I'm not going to argue about it." Then disengage and walk away. If you don't, the child will try to explain his way out of doing the task until you give in or get mad. If you find it necessary to

stay in the room, completely ignore the child's complaining. When you walk away or totally ignore the complaining, it sends a message that this matter is not up for negotiation. It also sends the message that you have complete confidence that your child will get the task done.

5. Don't give in. This is very important. If you say, "When you have picked up all the dog poop, then we'll leave for soccer practice," stay firm. If it's time to go to soccer practice and his task isn't finished, then you must follow through and delay going until the task is done. This won't happen often. He'll soon come to know when you say something, you really mean it.

Here are some examples of When-Then statements:

When you clean up your toys, **then** you can watch your show.

When you unload the dishwasher, **then** you can go outside and play with your friends.

When you've finished your homework and I've checked it, **then** we can leave for football practice.

When you've finished your family jobs, **then** you can facebook with your friends.

When you wash your hands, **then** you may eat.

When you stop whining, **then** I will listen to you.

When your dishes are in the dishwasher, **then** you may have dessert.

When you put your helmet on, **then** you may ride your bike.

Set Up a When-Then Bedtime Routine

Use a When-Then statement to set up a bedtime routine that will happen regularly every night. After your kids have completed all of the "When" tasks, then they can enjoy a normally occurring privilege until they have to get into bed. This is a good way to get kids into bed without nagging and reminding. Your When-Then statement will include a deadline: "When your teeth are brushed and your pajamas are on, then we can read bedtime stories. But at 8:00, lights out." If the kids are ready for bed at 7:50, they get 10 minutes of bedtime stories. Ready at 7:59 means one minute of bedtime stories. After that, lights out. Consider making a list of tasks that need to be accomplished to get ready for bed, and displaying it where each child can see it. "WHEN everything on the list is done, THEN you can watch TV until bedtime."

In order for kids to get the sleep they need, try to keep bedtime consistent every night of the week. If bedtime is at 8:00, stick to that time every night, even on the weekends. For children too young to tell time, use a timer to let them know that bedtime is when the timer goes off, and story time is over. If you are consistent and make bedtime a routine, you will have less trouble getting your kids into bed and less trouble getting them up in the morning.

Set Up a When-Then Morning Routine

Use a When-Then statement to set up a morning routine that will happen regularly every morning before school. After your kids have completed all of the "When" tasks, then they can enjoy a normally occurring privilege until they have to leave for school.

Once again, your When-Then statement will include a deadline and go something like this: "When you are dressed, your hair is brushed, your bed is made, your lunch is in your lunch box, your backpack is by the door, and your hands are washed, then you may eat breakfast. The kitchen, however, closes at 7:45 so you can get to the school bus on time."

Your child may have to be rushed out the door with a piece of toast and a banana, but after the first time, it will likely not happen again. If breakfast is not something your child gets excited over, choose another appropriate "Then", such as morning playtime, computer time, or TV time. Consider making a list of tasks that need to be accomplished each morning, and displaying it where each child can see what they need to do. "WHEN everything on the list is done, THEN you can Facebook."

The night before you start your first When-Then morning routine, sit down with your children and explain how the morning is going to unfold. Use your When-Then statement. Explain how they can expect the same routine every school morning. Soon your When-Then routine will become a routine and you won't have to remind your children anymore.

When-Then Tips

Make sure to use "when" and not "if." "If you feed the dog, then you can go play." "If" implies you are not confident the child will get the job done.

After saying your When-Then statement, you don't need to give reminders. But if the child does not do the "when," then you must deny the privilege. This may be hard on you, but you must remain firm if your child is going to take you seriously.

If you cannot think of a normally occurring privilege to go with your "then," choose another technique. Avoid denying a privilege that is not timely, such as: "When you clean your room then you can go to the birthday party tomorrow afternoon. In a case like this, you would be better off saying, "Son, I noticed your room needs to be cleaned and I also know that tomorrow you're planning to go to a birthday party. I'd like your room to be clean before you go, okay?" Then when your child says to you, "Bye, I'm going to the party," you can say, "WHEN your room is clean, THEN you can go to the party."

If your child totally disregards your When-Then, use other options like problem-solve together (Chapter 20) or consequences (Chapter 21).

19

Sibling Rivalry

Sibling rivalry can be caused by a number of reasons.

When a child sees her sibling receive the attention, approval and love that she should be receiving, she becomes jealous. Add to that the envy she feels for the accomplishments of another child, and the resentment she feels for privileges another brother or sister receives, and it all adds up to mean the sibling is perceived to be worth more. And if the sibling is worth more, then the child concludes that she must be worth less, and that is a problem.

Another cause of sibling rivalry is a child's need to feel superior, in charge, or empowered. If you are not helping to meet your child's need for a sense of personal power in positive ways, she will seek after it in negative ways such as teasing, bullying, or tormenting a brother or sister.

Other reasons for fighting among siblings might be that one child feels she was unjustly treated by her parents and takes it out on her brother or sister. Sometimes a child has had a bad day and a sibling gets the brunt of it. Sometimes disagreements between siblings erupt in a fight. There is always an underlying cause of bickering and fighting, and that cause is usually not obvious.

The 5 Principles discussed in Section 1 will go a long way toward helping you meet your children's basic needs of belonging and personal power in positive ways, thus reducing sibling rivalry.

Sometimes parents unintentionally promote sibling rivalry by doing the following:

Give more attention to one child than to another, or play favorites

Make a child share his possessions (toys or whatever)

Label a child: "Becki is the artistic one in the family."

Compare children: "Jimmy, if you would just apply yourself more like your sister does."

Asking kids to compete: "Let's see who can clean their room the fastest."

Reacting to Sibling Rivalry

It's understandable to feel that the aggressor in a sibling dispute should not get away with bad behavior and that the victim should be made to feel better, but it's also important to remember that the home is where kids should learn to solve problems. I'm going to provide you with some techniques to use, but before you get involved in a sibling dispute, ask yourself if you really need to get involved. Remember, your main objective should be to guide your children to work it out; to solve their own problems, and sometimes doing nothing is the best thing.

However, if you feel you must get involved, the first thing you need to do is acknowledge the negative feelings of both parties (as explained in Chapter 6). When you acknowledge negative feelings, your children are able to calm down, let go of their negative feelings, and often come up with ideas to solve the problem that caused their negative feelings.

Here are three levels of sibling conflict with a recommended response for each.

Level 1. Siblings are disagreeing or arguing.

Intervention is not needed. Ignore. Let the children work it out themselves.

Level 2. Siblings are shouting. The situation is heating up.

Intervention would be helpful.

Step 1. Stop the fighting and acknowledge their anger: "Hold it, you guys! You two sound really mad at each other."

Step 2. Allow them to vent, one at a time. "What's going on? Andrea, you first, then, when she's done, Kimmie, I want to hear from you." Give each child a chance to vent; to express her point of view without interruption from you or the other child – whether what she says is true or not. Remember, you are not to agree or disagree. The only thing you want to do in this step is let them *feel heard.*

Step 3. Reflect the point of view from each child. "So Andrea, you want to play by yourself without Kimmie tagging along. Kimmie, you have nothing to do, so you want to play with Andrea." In this step your objective is to let them *feel understood.*

Step 4. Summarize the problem. "That's a tough one. One of you wants to be left alone, and the other wants to play together."

Step 5. Express confidence that the two of them can work it out. "I'm confident that the two of you will come up with a solution that is fair for both of you. I'm going to let you two decide what to do." In this step you let them know that you do not intend to solve their problem, but have confidence they can solve the problem together.

You might think you haven't done anything to solve the problem, but you have. By letting each child feel heard and understood, you have enabled them to let go of their negative feelings and have given them the freedom to come up with solutions to the problem on their own.

What if the kids don't have the slightest idea about how to work it out? In that case you could offer one or two simple solutions: "One solution might be to arrange a time to play together later today or, Andrea, you could find something else for Kimmie to do so you can play by yourself. You guys talk it over."

If they still have a hard time coming to an agreement, you can try using the Either-Or statement (see Chapter 21). "Either you both work it out or I'll give you both something to do, and you may or may not like it." "Either you find a way so you can both play with the blocks or we will put them away for the rest of the day." "Either decide on a movie you can both watch or there won't be any movie."

What if they try to work it out and go back to shouting at each other? Then separating them might be the best option. You could say something like this: "Okay, one of you may not like what I'm going to say, but I'm going to decide who gets what. Andrea, you continue playing. Kimmie, you come keep me company. Then tonight we are going to have a meeting and decide what to do if one person is playing and the other person wants to play too."

Level 3. Physical harm has happened or is imminent, or something has or is about to get broken.

The situation demands your attention.

Step 1: Stop the fighting and describe what you see. "Hold it, you guys! I see two very angry children who are about to hurt each other."

Step 2: Separate the children. Say, "It's not safe to be together. I won't permit hurting one another. We need a cooling-off period. You. Go to your room. And you, go to yours."

Sometimes you can't ignore your children's squabbles and expect your children to figure out what to do on their own. You need to teach them. So, when everyone is calm, perhaps at your weekly family meeting (see Chapter 5) come together and teach your children how to handle disagreements. Consider covering the following points:

As for play-wrestling, decide on a word or phrase that one child can say during play-wrestling that will let the other child know that it is time to stop. A phrase like "stop now" lets the aggressor know that it is time to stop. However, a child who seeks a sense of personal power through wrestling or bullying will be slow to obey that rule. Section 1 teaches how to give children a sense of personal power in positive ways so they do not desire to seek it in negative ways.

Teach what causes bad feelings and to avoid them: name-calling, endless teasing, hitting, pushing, taking toys without asking, and arguing. Ask the children what causes bad feelings. They'll tell you.

Teach that either party can choose to walk away from a fight and put an end to it right then and there, and that good things come to those who patiently wait. For example, "He'll get tired of jumping on the trampoline after a while and you'll be able to have it all to yourself."

Teach the benefit of taking turns: "If you'll let me play with it for 10 minutes, then you can have it for 10 minutes and we'll take turns."

Teach when, and how to use "I feel" statements as described in chapter 16.

Teach how to make respectful requests rather than making demands or just taking what you want. Teach how saying "please," and "thank you," can go a long way in getting what you want. "Please, may I have my toy back?"

Teach that if you want something someone else has, try trading something for it.

Tattling

Often, a child will come to you in distress because of a squabble with a sibling. Acknowledging negative feelings like you would whenever a child comes to you in distress. Then follow the advice in Chapter 9 where it talks about problem-solving and handing the problem back to the child. Use these steps as a guideline:

1. Acknowledge negative feelings. Listen and let the child know you understand. "Ohhh no, that's gotta make you mad."
2. Hand the problem back. "What do you think you're going to do?"
3. Get permission to share ideas. "Would you like to hear what some other kids have tried?" Or, "Would you like some ideas?"

4. Provide a few ideas. "Some kids decide to _____. How would that work for you?" "Some kids decide to go somewhere else to play. How would that work for you?" "Some kids decide to help their dad rake leaves, and guess what? I just happen to be raking leaves. How would that work for you?"

5. Allow the child to choose the solution. "Well if anybody can figure it out, you can. Let me know how it goes."

When kids come running to you with complaints about a sibling and you let them feel heard and understood, you give them freedom to solve their own problems, and often, they will end up solving their problems on their own.

In their bestselling book, *Siblings without Rivalry*[1], authors Adele Faber and Elaine Mazlish describe how quickly parents should get in and out of sibling fights. They say, "Basically we try not to interfere, but when we must step in, it's always with the thought that at the earliest possible moment we want to turn the children back to dealing with each other. That's the best preparation we can give them for the rest of their lives."

By teaching your children how to solve problems between themselves and staying out of their fights, you empower them to figure things out on their own, a skill they will use the rest of their lives. It also releases you from the burden of having to be a judge and jury for every sibling argument.

Here's one more suggestion. Just like adults, sometimes kids need time by themselves. Make arrangements so that each child can occasionally have their own space and time to play with toys, by themselves or with a friend, without a sibling tagging along and without having to share with anyone.

20

Problem-Solve Together

The ability to solve problems is one of the greatest gifts you can give your children. It is a life-skill and comes with some nice benefits. Besides helping children solve their own problems, it helps them develop self-confidence, which contributes to their sense of personal power. The ability to solve problems, however, does not come naturally and must be taught. This chapter teaches how you and your children can solve problems together, particularly, behavior problems.

Before we go through the steps, I want to compare "consequences" with problem-solving to give you a sense that problem-solving should be tried before imposing consequences.

Let me illustrate with an example. Suppose you have a behavior problem that requires some correcting. Every weekday morning your 12-year-old daughter needs to be ready for school and in the car by 8 o'clock. If that happens, then you can get her to school on time and you can get to work on time. The problem is, your daughter is rarely ready on time. This causes you to have to race through traffic and you end up starting your work day all stressed out. You want to be able to enjoy your commute without the hassle of racing the clock.

Consequences

Let's take a look at how you would use consequences to put an end to this behavior problem. First, you'll need to think up a consequence that would "motivate" your child to be all ready for school and in the car by 8 o'clock. Then if she failed to do so, you would have to follow through with the consequence. You can think of at least three possible consequences:

1. Drive away at 8 o'clock and leave her home. This would require an adult to be with her; someone who could drive her to school when and if she finally got ready. She would surely feel the ire from her teacher for being late.

2. Take her to school in whatever condition she was in at 8 o'clock. If that meant that her backpack wasn't packed, or her hair not brushed, or she couldn't find a shoe, too bad. She would surely feel embarrassed when you kick her out of the car and her schoolmates catch a glimpse of her with ratty hair and only one shoe.

3. Take away a privilege. Confiscate her cell phone, ground her, or prohibit her from attending that long-anticipated birthday party this weekend. That might do the trick.

Let's take a look at what has happened. You have focused on her past behavior with the intention of making her "pay" if her behavior doesn't change. Your consequences are designed to hurt, and could feel very much like punishments. She does not learn *how* to change her behavior, only that her current behavior is displeasing.

Please understand, there is a time to use consequences, and you'll learn more about that in the next chapter. What I'm suggesting is, before you resort to using consequences, consider trying problem-solving first.

Problem-Solving

Problem-solving focuses on how to change behavior; what needs to be done in order to make things right. Consequences teach that bad choices result in pain. Problem-solving teaches that you can prevent problems by making different choices.

Back to our story.

Before you decide to use consequences, you decide to try problem-solving. So you have a one-on-one discussion with your daughter in the evening when you are both calm. You'll be using these three steps:

1. Find out how the child feels about the behavior in question

2. Identify some problems that the behavior causes

3. Talk about solutions

You: "Honey, I've asked you to be ready for school and in the car by 8 o'clock. How do you feel about that?" (Step 1)

Daughter: Is quiet for a few moments while she gathers her thoughts, and then says, "There's just so much to do to get ready."

You: "I'll bet that can be frustrating."

Daughter: "Yeah."

You: "What problems do you think it might cause when we are late getting out of here?"

Daughter: Shrugs her shoulders.

You: "It causes me to have to rush to get to work on time, and when that happens I get to work all stressed and I don't like that.

Besides, I have to drive like a maniac and that can't be safe." (Step 2)

Daughter: Tries to hold back a smile as she imagines you driving like a maniac.

You: "What can you and I do to solve this problem?" (Step 3)

Daughter: Shrugs her shoulders.

You: "I just want to work out a solution together and I think you might have some good ideas. What do you think about making a list of everything you need to do to get ready for school? I think we might both be surprised at how much there is.

You and your daughter brainstorm and make a list of everything she needs to do. She writes it down.

You: "Can you think of anything else?"

Daughter: "Wow, that's a lot."

You: "Now the question is, how are you going to get it all done in time to go?"

Daughter: "Well, I guess some of the stuff I can do the night before."

So you break the list into two parts: Part 1) The things she can do the night before, and part 2) the things she will do the morning of.

You: "How long do you think it will take you to do all the morning stuff?"

Daughter: "Not too long."

You are pretty sure she is underestimating how long it will take, but you feel this is a mistake she can learn from, so rather than trying to convince her to move some morning tasks to the night before, you say, "Let's give it a try and see how it goes. Can we get together again tomorrow night and talk about how things went?" She agrees.

The next night the two of you meet up.

You: "So how do you think it went this morning?"

Daughter: Well, I was in the car by 8 o'clock but I had to put on my makeup in the car and it was a hassle. I'm going to make some adjustments to the list and see what happens tomorrow."

Let's take a look at what happened.

Step 1. You began your conversation by asking her how she felt about being in the car by 8 o'clock. Then you reflected her feelings back: "I'll bet that can be frustrating." By doing that, you met her need to be heard and understood. That gave her the freedom to let go of her negative feelings and be open to solving the problem.

Step 2. Then you asked her what problems it might cause to leave after 8 o'clock. Asking questions encourages children to think. Then you explained the problem and told her how running late made you feel. You didn't blame or criticize. By expressing yourself in such a respectful, but assertive manner, she didn't feel a need to go on the defense or shut down.

Step 3. Then you asked her what you and she could do to solve the problem. By including yourself, she doesn't have to feel alone with this problem and she can consider you to be part of the solution. You expressed confidence in her ability to offer some good ideas. Encouragement like this makes kids feel good about getting involved. You followed that with a question: "What do you think about making a list...?" You started to guide her through the problem-solving process without "telling." Asking questions is the key to helping children think and explore ideas.

Then you brainstormed together and made a list of all the things she needs to do to be ready for school. After the list was complete, you asked, "Now the question is, how are you going to get it all done in time to go?" Another question that caused her to think. It was her idea to break the list into two parts: Part 1) The things she can do the night before, and part 2) the things she will need to do the morning of.

Then you continued to guide her through the process by asking, "How long do you think it will take you to do all the morning stuff?" When she said, "Not too long," you were tempted to say, "I don't think you can get all that stuff done by 8 o'clock," but you wisely held your tongue. You knew that she would learn more from her mistakes and errors in judgement than from anything you could say, so you said, "Let's give it a try and see how it goes." You also suggested that you meet up the next night to discuss how things went. It is important to follow up because it shows that you care, and it gives her a chance to be accountable for her choices. She agreed.

How do you think she feels? Now she's psyched to try her new plan. Is your *relationship* still intact? Yes, in fact it has probably strengthened. Were you able to *teach* her the behavior you expected? Yes. You taught her by asking questions and guiding her through the process of problem-solving. Did you *correct* her behavior? No. Actually, she corrected her own behavior. Then when you had your meet-up the next day, she made her own adjustments based on the experience she had that morning.

You met her need for a sense of personal power. I'm not so sure consequences meet that need – certainly not at the level problem-solving does. Problem-solving is also a skill that will serve your daughter throughout her life. She will use it to solve her own problems and then teach her own children how to solve their problems. Let's apply these three steps to a different problem.

Step 1 – Find out how the child feels about the behavior in question

First identify the behavior you want to talk about and then get your child's opinion on the matter. "I notice the dishes aren't getting done when it's your turn."

At this point your child may launch into her defense in which case you will listen. Or, she may remain quiet, in which case you will ask: "How do you feel about that?" Then listen. We've learned that only after a child believes that you understand what he or she is feeling, does that child care at all about listening to what YOU want to say. Use the skills you learned in Chapter 6 – Acknowledge Negative Feelings. If the child simply shrugs her shoulders and looks down, let her know you just want to work out a solution together and you think she might have some good ideas.

Step 2 – Identify some problems that the behavior causes

Ask, "What problems do you think that might cause?" or "What problems do you think it causes when you don't do your dishes when it's your turn?" After the child takes her turn, it's your turn. "It also causes some bad feeling for someone who wants to use a dish that hasn't been washed."

Step 3 – Talk about solutions

Ask, "What can you and I do to solve this problem?" That's right. Ask your child to involve you in coming up with a solution. Be prepared to write all suggestions down. Better yet, have the child write all the suggestions down. "Let's make a list of possible solutions." Don't prejudge or evaluate any suggestions at this point. You might be surprised to find that your child will come up with possible solutions that you haven't thought of.

After you have listed all possible solutions, go through the list together and eliminate those that would not work for whatever reason. "Now let's go through the list and decide what we want to keep and what we want to toss out."

Here is an example of Dad problem-solving with his son:

Dad: "Can we talk?" as he knocked on Tommy's bedroom door.

Tommy: "I'm kind of in the middle of something."

Dad: "Okay, then I'll get right to it. I notice the dishes aren't getting done when it's your turn."

Tommy: "Dad, I hate it when I have to empty the dishwasher, I hate to wash the pots and pans after the food has dried on them. I hate having to bring dishes over from the table, I hate having to scrape other people's plates, and I hate putting food away."

Dad: "Wow. I had no idea. That must be totally overwhelming."

Tommy: "Yeah. It's easier to not do them and get in trouble than do them and be mad the whole time."

Dad: "I can see how that would make you not want to do the dishes. What problems do you think it might cause when the dishes don't get done?"

Tommy: "To be honest, I really don't care."

Dad: Not wanting to get into an argument, he continues to step 3. "I see. Do you think together we could find a way to make the job of dishes not seem so overwhelming? I think you might have some good ideas and I'd like to hear them."

Tommy: "Yeah, whatever."

Dad and Tommy made a list of possible solutions:

1. Take Tommy off dishes duty - forever.
2. Create a new job on the job chart for emptying the dishwasher.
3. Ask whoever is cooking to rinse the pots and pans after using them.
4. Ask everyone to bring their plates from the table, scrape them into the garbage, rinse them in the sink, and put them in the dishwasher.
5. Ask everyone to help put all the food away after each meal.

This is the end of the story. I'll let you guess which possible solutions they kept and which they scratched off. Can you add anything to the list? Do you think your children can add anything to the list?

Let's look at a few different ways a father might handle a problem with his teenage son who is supposed to come home by 11:00 p.m., but doesn't come home until 1:00 a.m. The father might threaten by saying, "You keep that up and you won't take the car again." Or, he might use guilt to persuade his son to comply with the rule: "Your mother and I worry about you when you don't come home on time. Don't do that to us again." Or, the father might impose a punishment: "Son, we had an agreement that you could use the car if you were in by eleven and you haven't kept your end of the agreement. You're grounded from the car for a week." None of these discipline methods teach the son to take responsibility for his actions or make him comply because he wants to please his father.

Let's see how this father could use problem-solving with his son to address his son's behavior. Before this type of problem-solving can happen, the father and son must already have a good relationship and they must have already agreed on the expectation for his son to be in by 11:00 p.m. Notice that the father doesn't focus on the fact that the son came in late. He focuses on a deeper issue: trust. He also addresses the situation in a way that doesn't erode the relationship.

Father: "Son, I know it's important to you to be trusted—isn't that right?

Son: "Yeah."

Father: "And I want to trust you. But I have to tell you that when we both agree that you'll come in at eleven and you don't come in until one a.m., I trust you less. I don't like feeling that way. I want to feel that I can totally trust you. What can both of us do that will make us feel good about your use of the car?"

Son: "Dad, It's unreasonable to expect me to come in at eleven. None of my friends have to."

Father: "I understand that you feel it isn't fair, and I want it to be fair for both of us. I get worried about you *and* the car when you're out past eleven. What can we do that will make us feel good about this situation?"

They will work on the solution until they can come to an agreement. Perhaps they can compromise on a time to be home, or agree that the son will text with his location and estimated time of arrival if he's going to be late. If the father taught his son to make wise decisions, he must learn to trust his son when he can't watch over him. That's hard for a Dad to do. Likewise, the son needs to understand that it is just natural for a father to worry about his son when his son doesn't come home by an agreed upon time. That's hard for a teenager to do.

Problem-Solve at Family Meetings

Family meetings are an ideal place to teach problem-solving. You can guide children in a group setting to solve problems regarding their behavior the same way you guide them one-on-one. Just go through the three steps.

Summary of the Problem-Solving Process:

1. Find out how the child feels about the behavior in question

Explain the behavior that is displeasing.

Ask "How do you feel about that?"

Acknowledge negative feelings.

2. Identify some problems that the behavior causes

Ask, "What problems do you think it might cause when…"

Identify problems that haven't been addressed.

3. Talk about solutions

Ask, "What can we do to solve this problem?"

Optional: "I just want to work out a solution together and I think you might have some good ideas."

Invite the child to write down all possible solutions. Allow him to make suggestions before you make yours. Make your suggestions into a question: "What do you think about…?

Talk about the best solutions on the list and when to start implementing them.

Then decide when you are going to meet-up to talk about how it went.

21

Consequences

We learn from our mistakes. Another way to put that is, *we learn from the consequences that result from making poor choices.* The lessons we learn from consequences are more powerful and memorable than any instructions or warnings we could receive.

Consequences and punishment are not the same. Where consequences provide learning experiences, punishment promotes anger and resentment. More on that later. There are two types of consequences, natural consequences and logical consequences.

Natural Consequences

Natural consequences are results of choices we make without intervention from anyone else. For example, forgetting to put ice cream in the freezer results in melted ice cream. Staying too long in the sun results in a sunburn. Eating too much candy results in a stomach ache. As adults, we experience a natural consequence *every time* we make a choice. Natural consequences can be positive or negative depending on the choices we make.

Kids make choices too. Poor choices result in physical or emotional pain. So parents spend a good deal of time trying to keep their kids from making poor choices. "Stay out of the street," "Stay away from the pool," "don't touch the burner on the stove," "Eat breakfast," "Don't forget your lunch," "Do your homework."

All these *rules* have an undesirable natural consequence attached if they are not followed.

Natural consequences are powerful ways to learn, but allowing children to learn from natural consequences is not always practical. You tell your children to stay out of the street because the natural consequence could be getting hit by a car. You teach them to brush their teeth because the natural consequence would be getting cavities. You instruct them to stay close to you at the store because the natural consequence might be getting lost or hurt or getting in the way of other shoppers. But children do not have the foresight or the knowledge to avoid making poor choices that could result in unacceptable natural consequences. So parents come up with *logical* consequences; consequences that replace the unacceptable natural consequences.

Logical Consequences

Logical consequences can be positive or negative. Children behave well to enjoy the positive consequences of behaving well. Giving attention to good behavior, as discussed in Chapter 13, is all about providing positive logical consequences. Negative logical consequences are substitutes for negative natural consequences with the intent of preventing the natural consequence from ever happening.

The natural consequence of not brushing teeth is getting cavities. Since you don't want your children to experience this natural consequence, you make a rule with a logical consequence: "Kids, I'm concerned about your teeth. I don't want you to get cavities and I know that brushing teeth helps prevent cavities. I want you to brush your teeth every night before bed. I also know that sweets like candy and desserts help give you cavities. So, if you do not brush your teeth every night before bed, there will be no sweets; no candy, no desserts, no treats of any kind. Now, just so I know you understand, can you please tell me what I just said?"

No need to remind the kids after that. The next day, have ice cream for dessert. "Okay, you may have some ice cream if you brushed your teeth last night. Sam? Oh, no. Billy, you didn't brush your teeth last night." Say no more. Let the consequence do the teaching. Do not let Billy's anger or tears make you cave in. Tomorrow night, have chocolate chip cookies.

The advantage of using logical consequences is that a child does not like the "pain" associated with the consequence and you usually have to enforce the consequence only once or twice before the child decides to consistently obey the rule. The consequence does all the teaching so you don't have to. You *do not* have to say anything like, "See? I told you what would happen, didn't I?" or "I hope you learned your lesson."

The down side to logical consequences is that they can easily become disguised as punishments. In his book, Children: The Challenge[1], Rudolf Dreikurs says, "When we use the term 'logical consequences,' parents so frequently misinterpret it as a new way to impose their demands upon children. The children see this for what it is – disguised punishment." Here are the four steps to make logical consequences separate from punishments:

1. Decide on an appropriate consequence
2. Explain the rule with the consequence
3. Allow the child to break the rule
4. Deliver the consequence

Let's take a closer look at each of these steps.

Step 1. Decide on an appropriate consequence

First, determine the *natural* consequence. Would the natural consequence be the appropriate consequence? Perhaps going through the embarrassment of not completing the school science project on time would be an appropriate natural consequence. If a natural consequence is not practical, then decide on a logical consequence. Use the following four guidelines to decide on an appropriate logical consequence:

1. Related to the rule. If a child makes a mess, the related consequence would be to have the child clean up the mess. If a child comes in after curfew, a related consequence would be suspended use of the car.

2. Reasonable (not too harsh). If a child makes a mess, cleaning the entire house would be considered an unreasonable consequence.

3. Revealed in advance. This helps the child understand that his poor choice is the bad guy, not the parents.

4. Repeated back. Make sure the child is clear on the rule, the reason for the rule, and what will happen if the rule is broken.

If you cannot think of a logical consequence that conforms to these four guidelines, then don't use this technique because your logical consequence will feel more like a punishment. Following is a list of rules along with their associated natural consequences and possible logical consequences. Notice that for some rules, the natural consequence is the best consequence.

Rule: Wear your bicycle helmet.
Natural Consequence: You might fall and hurt your head.

Logical Consequence: You lose the privilege of riding your bike.

Rule: Stay next to me at the supermarket.
Natural Consequence: You might get lost or hurt or get in the way of other shoppers.
Logical Consequence: You will ride in the shopping cart, wait in the car with an adult, or immediately go home and not be invited to come next time.

Rule: Do not go near the pool.
Natural Consequence: You might fall in and drown.
Logical Consequence: You will stay inside.

Rule: Do your homework.
Natural Consequence: You will get bad grades.
Logical Consequence: You don't go anywhere or do anything until it's done and I check it.

Rule: Don't leave your bike on the driveway.
Natural Consequence: Mom or Dad can't park the car in the garage and the bike might get run over.
Logical Consequence: You lose your bike-riding privileges.

Rule: You have a half hour to clean your room.
Natural Consequence: Messy rooms are stinky and unsightly.
Logical Consequence: I will put the stuff left out in a box and the only way to get your stuff back is to earn it back by doing extra jobs around the house.

Rule: Give yourself enough time to eat breakfast.
Natural Consequence: You will be hungry until lunch.
Logical Consequence: None.

Rule: Remember to take your lunch.

Natural Consequence: You will be hungry until snack-time or dinner.
Logical Consequence: None.

Rule: Don't tip over your glass of milk.
Natural Consequence: You will have to clean it up.
Logical Consequence: None.

Rule: Sit still in your seat while we are at a restaurant.
Natural Consequence: You will disturb other customers and anger the restaurant staff.
Logical Consequence: You will wait in the car with a parent until everyone else gets done eating.

Step 2. Explain the Rule with the Consequence

Once you have come up with an appropriate natural or logical consequence, you can explain the rule with the consequence attached:

1. Explain the rule.
2. Explain the 'why' behind the rule
3. Explain the logical consequence
4. Have the child repeat back what you said

Step 3. Allow the Child to Break the Rule

After the rule has been properly set, you are done until the child breaks the rule. No need to nag, remind or lecture about obeying the rule. Simply allow the child to break the rule and let your logical, or natural, consequence do the teaching.

Billy says, "I'm going to go ride my bike. See ya." You notice his bicycle helmet on the kitchen table. What do you do? Do you yell, "Billy, don't forget your helmet!" No. This will train Billy to depend on you to remind him whenever he forgets and you can't always be there to remind him. Do you grab his helmet and run it out to him? Don't you dare. Instead, watch Billy. If he gets on his bike and makes that first push on his peddle, carry out the consequence. After getting Billy's attention, do Step 4.

Step 4. Deliver the Consequence

There are three parts to effectively delivering a consequence:

1. **Express a sense of sadness for the decision your child just made.** "Ohh noo." By saying this, Billy becomes aware that his *bad choice* is the bad guy, and not you. This is only effective when you set the rule and reveal the consequence in advance.

2. **Explain what you see.** "I see you riding without your helmet."

3. **Carry out the consequence with respect.** Point to the garage and say, "Garage."

No need to say, "Hey, remember we talked about what would happen if you didn't wear your helmet." Or, "If you would have worn your helmet, this would never have happened." In fact, the less you say the better. It will sound something like this: "Hey Billy. Billy, wait! Ohh noo. I see you not wearing your helmet. Garage," as you point to the garage.

Billy might try to talk you out of it: "Oh, man. I totally forgot. Please can I have another chance? Pleeease?" This is where your love for Billy and his safety take a higher priority than your desire to make him happy by giving into his begging. You know that if you give him one more chance you take away a learning opportunity AND you teach him that if he whines enough, he can get you to change your mind. So you shake your head and say, "I'm sorry, Billy," meaning, I'm sorry you made a poor choice.

You're at the restaurant. Your daughter knows that the "restaurant rule" says, "Stay in your seat at the restaurant or be taken to the car by an adult where you both will wait until everyone else is done eating." However, she has chosen to run around instead of stay in her seat. "Ohh no," you say in a sad voice. "I see you running around. You and I need to go sit in the car." When your children hear you say, "Ohh no," they will quickly come to realize they made a bad decision.

Here is an example of a father setting a rule with a consequence. The son is dribbling his basketball in the house:

Dad: "Hey son, Come here. I'm afraid that dribbling your basketball in the house will hurt the floor, and besides that, it's really annoying."

Son: "It won't hurt the floor."

Dad: Treats the response like annoying behavior and ignores it. "From now on, if you dribble your basketball in the house, I will remind you by taking your basketball."

Son: "Seriously?"

Dad: That's all I wanted to tell you.

Son: "What? That's a bunch of crap."

Dad: Says nothing.

Son: "What if I forget and accidentally dribble it?

Dad: "I guess you'll find out."

Son: "Fine!" and stomps away.

If the son continues to argue, the dad can calmly say, "I'm not going to argue about it." If the son still continues to argue, the dad can walk away. Notice that Dad ignored anything the boy said that wasn't an effort to clarify the rule or the consequence.

After the rule and consequence have been explained, Dad will look for good behavior and give it attention. "Son, I noticed you didn't dribble your basketball in the house all day. Thank you." The next day however, the son is caught dribbling the basketball in the house.

Dad: "Ohh no. I see you dribbling your basketball."
Son: "Oh my gosh, really?"
Dad: "I'll take that, thank you."
Son: Throws Dad the ball and walks away mad.
Dad: Treats his son's remark as annoying behavior and ignores it. Dad does not say, "Hey, I warned you," or, "It was your choice." He keeps the ball for 10 minutes, then finds his son and tosses him the ball. Not a word is said. It might be noteworthy that dad hated to cause his son pain, but knew that the consequence of losing the basketball would teach his son better than any reminder, lecture, or threat.

Consequences speak so much louder than words. No need to say, "Try to remember from now on," or, "Next time it will be longer." If the incident happens again, Dad will take the ball for an hour. Then, the next time it happens, maybe all day. It won't be long before the son knows that Dad will follow through with the consequence every time. After a couple of days of obeying the rule, Dad gives attention to the good behavior again: "Son, I've noticed you haven't dribbled in the house for two days. Thank you." When the son replies with, "Whatever," the dad ignores it as he would any annoying remark.

The Difference between Consequences and Punishments

There's a difference between consequences and punishments. Punishments are about making kids suffer for their mistakes. They're usually intended to make kids feel so bad about their poor choice that they will never want to do it again. Punishments are often unrelated to the bad behavior and they may be severe in nature. Here are some examples of punishments:

A 5-year-old doesn't pick up his toys when he's told. He is spanked.

A 7-year-old talks back to his mother. She washes his mouth out with soap.

A 9-year-old misbehaves at school. His parents give him extra chores to do at home to "teach him a lesson."

A 13-year-old leaves his baseball glove in the driveway. His father purposely drives over it with the car.

A 16-year-old is caught lying. She is grounded for a week.

The problem with punishments is that they often cause children to feel bad about who they are — as opposed to what they did. Punishments diminish self-worth and weaken the relationship between children and parents.

Punishments do not cause children to think about how they can do better. Instead, they cause kids to focus their anger on their parents and compel them to plan how not to get caught next time. Punishments can actually motivate children to seek revenge. For example, instead of thinking, "I made a poor choice," the child might think, "You're mean. You can't tell me what to do. You think *that* behavior was bad, just watch." Punishments might seem to work in the short-term, but in the long-term, they do not promote good behavior.

Consequences, delivered properly, teach children to think that their poor choice was the bad guy instead of Mom and Dad, and teach children to reconsider their choice before breaking the rule again.

When I teach logical consequences, I am often asked to suggest a consequence for a particular situation. I tell them if they can't think of a logical consequence that meets the four guidelines then their situation probably does not call for a logical consequence. There are other methods of *correcting* that might be more effective such as:

Expressing how you feel
Offering choices
Setting up When-Then routines
Problem-solving together

If correcting isn't working, perhaps more attention needs to be given to *teaching*. Does the child understand the rule and why it was created? Are you giving positive attention to good behavior when it happens?

If misbehavior still persists, then you need to focus on building relationships. Are you spending enough one-on-one time with the child? Are you engaged in family activities, eating together and family meetings? Are you acknowledging negative feeling when the child is in distress? Are you getting to know your child's likes, dislikes, opinions, worries, desires, fears, wishes and beliefs? Are you making positive deposits in your child's life?

Either-Or

Use this technique to make a rule with a consequence in the heat of the moment when there is no time for teaching. Here is an example:

Mom has guests over and her son has been running through the house, back and forth, being a nuisance. She decides to use the Either-Or technique and says, "Brice, stop! Now listen, this is important. From now on, no running. EITHER you walk, OR you will spend 10 minutes in your room. You decide." That's it. Done.

Mom watches for good behavior so she can reinforce it by giving it attention: "Brice. I notice you've been walking." Then gives a thumbs-up.

If Brice runs through the house again, Mom will calmly say, "Brice, come here. I see you running." She points to his room and simply says, "Room. I will set my timer for 10 minutes. When it goes off, I will come get you." Mom will set her timer, make sure Brice goes to his room, and let the consequence do all the teaching.

Mom will not give in to pleadings: "But Mom, I promise I won't run again. I promise! Please?" If Mom gives in, she knows she will be teaching her child that pleading results in no consequence, and the next time (and there will be a next time) the pleadings will become louder and longer. When Mom goes to release Brice from his room, all she needs to say is, "Your 10 minutes are up." No need for warnings or lectures.

A mom is at the supermarket, shopping. Her child is running all around the store. "Son," she says to him, "No running around in the store. EITHER you stay by me OR you will sit in the cart." If the boy continues to run around, she will say, "I see you've decided to sit in the cart."

A family is dining out at a restaurant. Little Billy is running around. Dad says, "Billy, EITHER sit up to the table and stay there, OR you and I will go sit in the car." Dad has no need to follow up with, "And I mean it," because Billy knows from experience that Dad will do what he says.

Let me tell you an experience I had using Either-Or. During a family reunion at a campground, some of the smaller children wanted to go swimming at the pool. I volunteered to be the lifeguard. I was given strict instructions by my daughter-in-law to make sure her daughter (my granddaughter) wore her life jacket.

So there we were at the pool. I noticed my granddaughter playing in an inflatable donut, but she was not wearing her life jacket. I called out, "Put your life jacket on." "NO!" she replied. Hmmm. Now what do I do? I decided to use the Either-Or. After all, what could I lose? I called out again, "EITHER you put on your life jacket now, OR you get out of the pool and stay out." She said, "Okaaaay," like my request was really interfering with her pool time. I was relieved because I really didn't want to come up with a plan "C."

22

Tantrums

Tantrums are very obnoxious behaviors of young children, but are usually easy to eliminate. When a child has a tantrum, he screams, cries, falls to the floor, kicks, throws his arms around, and is almost impossible to ignore.

What Causes Tantrums?

Tantrums are usually caused by a child not getting what he wants. It works like this: A child wants something: a cookie right before dinner, for instance. His parent tells him "No." So, out of disappointment, the child cries. During one of those times, a parent says, "Okay, stop crying, here's a cookie." What has the child just learned? Crying equals cookie. Can you imagine what a marvelous discovery this is?

The parent doesn't want the child to get his way every time he cries, so the parent holds out, not giving in when the child asks for a cookie again. The child cries harder. Finally, the parent can't stand the noise any longer and gives the child what he wants.

The parent resolves not to give in the next time, but the child doesn't give up. The child has learned that crying long and loud equals cookie. You'd think that since all that screaming is so nerve-racking to adults, it would be irritating to the child after a while, but it never seems to be.

The longer and louder the tantrum lasts, the more apt the parent is to give into the child's demand. The child learns that he can use the same trick to get candy, toys, even his parent's undivided attention. And it works beautifully in stores, at church, and when visiting friends with Mom or Dad.

That's how tantrums get started. If a parent knows what to do, tantrums should never be a problem. Let's look at how you should deal with tantrums. There are three levels of tantrums:

1. Almost-tantrums

2. Small tantrums

3. Full-blown tantrums

Almost-tantrums

Almost-tantrums are whining, begging and crying. Never, ever, ever give a child what he wants when he is whining, begging or crying for it. Don't give in. Giving in will teach the child that he can get what he wants by whining, begging or crying. You can say, "When you can talk with a sweet voice, then I will talk with you." When the child calms down and begins asking in a "sweet voice", then engage in a conversation.

Small Tantrums

Small tantrums are just that, small tantrums. The child is not crying or kicking very hard and it looks like it might not last very long. Whatever you do, don't give the child what he wants.

Remember, the child is having a tantrum because he was able to get what he wanted in the past by acting this way. He's experimenting; seeing if he can reproduce the same result as before.

Full-Blown Tantrums

Full-blown tantrums are when the child does not hold back. He throws himself on the floor, kicks hard, screams loudly and seems to be out of control. The child has probably had success using tantrums before and is determined to outlast your resolve to not give in.

What to do

Give an Ignore Warning. While your child is calm, say, "Honey, I want to tell you something. You know how sometimes when you want something and I tell you 'No', and you feel mad and scream and cry and kick your legs? Well, from now on, when you do that, I'm going to ignore you. That means I will pretend that you are not there. It's not that I don't care, I do. And I'll be glad to talk with you after you're feeling better. So, next time you get mad and scream and cry and kick your legs, what am I going to do? That's right. I will ignore you. But I will still love you."

Give in fantasy what you cannot (or will not) give in reality. Think back to Chapter 6 when we learned a skill called: Give in fantasy. We can use this skill when the child whines, begs, cries or is about to throw a tantrum because he wants something he can't have. Stay very calm and give in fantasy what you cannot give in reality. After you say, "Sorry, no cupcakes before dinner," and the child goes into pre-tantrum mode, kneel down so you are at eye-level with your child and say:

"I hear you. You really wish you had a cupcake. That's gotta be disappointing. I hate it when I'm looking forward to eating something and I can almost taste it, and then find out I have to wait."

When a child feels heard and understood the odds increase that he will stop his whining, begging or launching a tantrum. If this doesn't help, then do the following:

Totally ignore the child. Stay calm. Pay no attention to him. Allow the child to kick and scream. Act as if you don't even know he is there. If he grabs your leg, free yourself with as little bother as possible. If the child is in a safe place, leave the room. Treat this as you would any annoying behavior.

Relocate the child if necessary. If you are at a store, in a restaurant, in church or any other public place, you may feel it necessary to relocate the screaming child. As inconvenient as it may be, remove the child to a safe place. If you are at a restaurant, you might have to sit in the car with your child until everyone else finishes eating. If at a store or church, you may have to go home. The child must come to realize that the tantrum is not going to get him what he wants.

As soon as kids learn that tantrums do not work, the tantrums will stop. Children will do only what works. If tantrums no longer work, there's really no reason to continue using them.

23

Seek Divine Guidance

I'm going to make some statements you may or may not agree with. However, I believe they are true and that you can benefit from them.

There is a God. He is an immortal, glorified, personal being. He created our spirits and is literally our father. I call him our Father in Heaven. We were created in His image. He sent our spirits to this earth to receive a physical body. He has spoken to people whom we call prophets. The prophets wrote what they learned and we call that scripture.

Our Heavenly Father has a son who we know as Jesus Christ. He received a physical body when His spirit was sent to this earth 2,000 years ago. If we are sons and daughters of Heavenly Father, then Jesus Christ is literally our brother. Now, I don't know any scripture that talks about this, but I believe we have a Heavenly Mother. I cannot imagine a Heavenly Father without a Heavenly Mother, can you? I won't speculate anymore here about a Heavenly Mother other than to say if she does exist, she must love us very much.

While I was writing this book, I wondered if the scriptures could guide you and I to be better parents. If Heavenly Father wanted to teach us how to be good parents, surely he would guide and direct us through scriptures. So as I studied the scriptures, I watched for teachings and examples that could be applied to parenthood, and tried to pattern my book after how I interpreted those scriptures. I believe my 3-Step Parenting Formula comes pretty close to what the scriptures teach us about being good parents. Here is how I perceive His guidance. We can pattern the way we parent our children by observing how our Heavenly Father parents us by observing these three steps:

Step 1. He loves us and He wants us to love him. In the Old Testament, in Deuteronomy 6:5, we read, "Thou shalt love the Lord thy God with all thine heart, and with all thy soul, and with all thy might." I interpret that to mean He wants to create a relationship with us – a strong relationship, and if we can do that, we will live his commandments and follow his teachings because we want to, and we will feel bad if we disappoint Him. *Step one: Heavenly Father wants us to have a strong relationship with Him.*

Step 2. He gives us commandments, or teachings that he wants us to follow. Some people consider his commandments to be too restrictive. I think just the opposite; that his commandments help us to avoid trouble and teach us to find purpose and meaning to our lives. The 10 Commandments are an example of his teachings. During the Last Supper, the Savior gave a new commandment to His Apostles. In St. John 13:34, we read, "A new commandment I give unto you, That ye love one another; as I have loved you, that ye also love one another." Heavenly Father teaches us through his Son, and our brother, Jesus Christ. He gave us Jesus Christ to be a model for us to follow. *Step two: Heavenly Father teaches us.*

Step 3. He knows that we're going to make mistakes and screw up from time to time. So he gives us a principle called repentance. Repentance is all about correcting our behavior and recommitting ourselves to obey His commandments and teachings. In St. Luke

24:47, we read, "And that repentance and remission of sins should be preached in his name among all nations, beginning at Jerusalem." Heavenly Father also blesses us to feel confused or distressed when we choose not to obey his teachings. *Step three: Heavenly Father corrects us.*

Here is something else I believe. Our Heavenly Father gives us a way to communicate *with* Him so we can get help *from* Him. In James 1:5, it says, "If any of you lack wisdom, let him ask of God, that giveth to all men liberally, and upbraideth not; and it shall be given him." That tells me that if we need divine inspiration about parenting, we can ask Him and He will either inspire us to know what to do, or guide us to find the knowledge we need.

I sought inspiration from our Heavenly Father as I wrote this book, and there were times when I noticed thoughts and words come into my mind. I feel I was led to find resources from which to draw information that parents need to know. I wanted every parent to benefit from this book, so I prayed continually, seeking divine inspiration to write a book worthy of the time parents will take to read it.

I consider this book to be one of the most important books that a parent will ever read. That's a huge responsibility so I wanted to get it right. I think this book has the potential to change the world by strengthening families.

I want Moms and Dads to know that parenting should not have to be bewildering, and parents do not have to resign themselves to a life of stress and frustration to raise children. Parents can experience joy and peace.

I have written this chapter to give you a peek into my life as an author and to convince you that as a parent, you have the ability to seek and receive divine guidance from your Heavenly Father as you raise your children. They are His children too, and so it would only make sense that He would help you to raise them to be good people.

Moving Forward

If you are experimenting with some of the teachings in this book, you are already strengthening your relationships with your children and discovering that it is easier to teach and correct them. You are noticing stress and frustration decreasing and peace of mind increasing.

You are strengthening your family. Your home is becoming a place of refuge, understanding, learning and love. Your children are adopting values to guide their lives, giving them greater self-esteem and more power to resist temptation.

I applaud you for your desire to improve you parenting skills. Your efforts will affect generations to come.

Here are some things to do moving forward.

Practice

Continue practicing what you've learned here. Practice implies that you're going to make mistakes. That's Okay. Just don't revert back to screaming, threatening, punishing, denying negative feelings or spending little or no quality time with your children. Keep working on strengthening your relationships because everything is built on that.

Spread the Word

You can make a difference in other people's lives by introducing them to The 3-Step Parenting Formula. Simply tell them about *3stepparenting.com* or give them the book, *3-Step*

Parenting as a gift. Can you imagine your friends and neighbors building stronger relationships with their children and teaching and correcting the 3-step parenting way? What a difference it could make in their lives. Please join me in telling others about how they can be 3-step parents.

Visit my Blog

There you will find things that uplift, inspire and enlighten. This is where subjects that have been left out of the book will be addressed. Go to *3stepparenting.com*.

Write a review

Your help in spreading the word is gratefully appreciated and reviews in places like Amazon.com make a big difference in helping new readers find this book.

About the Author

When I was a young parent, I had a reoccurring thought about being a parent. It went something like this: "What did I get myself into? This is not what I signed up for. If things don't change, I'm in trouble and so are my kids." You see, I figured that love and common sense and natural instincts were all I needed to raise children. I had observed other parents struggling to "control" their children, and I vowed that would never be me. My kids were going to be cooperative. You can guess what happened. Reality is a hard master. I came to understand and appreciate how those struggling parents felt as I joined their ranks.

I was frustrated by my children's behavior. I thought if I just hung in there and endured, things would change. Then something happened to make me realize that if my kids were going to change, I would have to change first.

One evening my wife, my two daughters (ages 2 and 4), and I were sitting down to dinner. As I remember, I was not in a good mood to begin with, and the drama and chaos at the dinner table was a little more than usual. One of the girls pointed to the other and said, "She has more mashed potatoes than I do." I don't know what made me do this, but my reaction was immediate. I put my hand into the bowl of mashed potatoes, scooped out a handful, and threw it down on her plate with a splat.

I said, "There, happy now?"

My daughter cried and I angrily left the table.

Up until then I was a nice guy; kind and considerate. Being a Dad had turned me into monster. I knew something had to change, and soon, before something worse happened.

Up to that point, I really didn't feel a need to learn parenting skills. After that, I was *obsessed* with learning parenting skills. I wanted to be a good dad but came to realize if I was going to be honest with myself, I couldn't do it without help. I would have to change, and changing meant learning to do things differently.

So I started reading books; a lot of books. Do you know how many parenting books are out there? There is no end. They taught different methods of parenting which was confusing, and in my opinion they all had one thing in common: they were complicated and difficult for me to understand. To this day I continue to read books about child behavior and I'm finding now that most of the information I read is a repeat from other books.

Fast forward many years. I have six children, all grown up, with families of their own. I often reflect back on those days when I was at the end of my rope as a parent. I wonder how many parents are in the same boat as I was in – wanting to make a change, but not knowing where to begin.

I think if I were in their shoes, here is what I would want. I would want a book that promises to bring out the best in me and my children. I would want that book to be short and to the point, easy to understand and easy to do. I would want it to be that *one* place I could go to get the answers that I needed without a lot of clutter to sift through. I know that parents don't have a lot of time to do research on child behavior, so I did the research for them, and wrote the book you are now holding.

It took me over a year to write this book. Often, my book would be the last thing I thought about before falling to sleep at night, and the first thing on my mind when I woke up in the morning. Sometimes I'd wake up in the middle of the night with a thought that I had to write down. I carried a pen and paper with me everywhere to capture the fleeting moments of inspiration.

I was constantly deciding what information to include in my book and what information to leave out. I struggled at putting into words exactly what I wanted to say. I'm not an eloquent writer.

As I see it, we're all in this raising-kids-thing together. We are the "village" helping each other raise children. It is my sincere hope that this book will give you the help that you've been looking for. Writing it has truly been a labor of love for me.

Richard O'Keef

Notes

Chapter 1

1 Washington Post, 2 June 1990, p. 2.

Chapter 3

1 Adapted from The Parenting Pyramid published by The Arbinger Institute, 1998

Chapter 5

1 Shannon Alder, *350 Questions Parents Should Ask During Family Night* (Cedar Fort Inc., 2018), p.9, 27, 38

Chapter 6

1 Adele Faber & Elaine Mazlish, *How To Talk So Kids Will Listen & Listen So Kids Will Talk* (New York: Scribner, 2012), p.42

Chapter 8

1 Stephen R. Covey, *The 7 Habits of Highly Effective Families* (New York: Golden Books, 1997), p. 45.

Chapter 9

1 Merrilee Brown Boyack, *The Parenting Breakthrough* (Deseret Book Company, 2005), p. 12.

Chapter 10

1 Adapted from a post written by Kristen Ulrich dated 1/25/17. See https://www.fearlessmotivation.com/2017/01/25/never-ever-give-up/.

Chapter 13

1 Dr. Glenn I. Latham, *The Power of Positive Parenting* (P & T ink, 1990), p. 9.

2 Paul Axtell, *Ten Powerful Things to Say to Your Kids: Creating the relationship you want with the most important people in your life* (Jackson Creek Press, 2011), p. 33-34.

Chapter 15

1 L. R. Knost, *Two Thousand Kisses a Day* (Little Hearts Books, LLC, 2013), p.49

2 Jane Nelsen, Ed.D., *Positive Discipline*, 3rd ed. (New York: Ballantine Books, 2006), p. 14.

3 Dale Carnegie, *How to Win Friends & Influence People* (New York: Pocket Books, 1936), p.5

Chapter 16

1 Dr. Haim G. Ginott, *Between Parent and Child* (New York: Three Rivers Press, 1965, Revised and updated by Dr. Alice Giinott and Dr. H. Wallace Goddard, 2003), p. 87.

Chapter 18

1 Amy McCready, *If I Have to Tell You One More Time* (New York: Penguin Group, 2012), p. 138.

Chapter 19

1 Adele Faber & Elaine Mazlish, *Siblings Without Rivalry* (New York: W. W. Norton& Company, Inc, 2012), p.157

Chapter 21

1 Rudolf Dreikurs and Vicki Soltz, *Children: The Challenge* (New York: Plume, 1964), p. 80

Recommended Books

During my research, I read a lot of books. Out of those books a few became my favorites. If you want to continue your study of how to be a better parent, these are my recommendations – in no particular order. All of these books can be found on Amazon.com.

If I Have to Tell You One More Time... by Amy McCready. The author examines why children misbehave and then presents 23 parenting skills with which parents can experiment. In Chapter 2 she introduces what she calls "Mind, Body & Soul Time," which is comparable to Chapter 4 in this book: "Spend One-On-One Time with Each Child." On page 35 she says, "Mind, body & Soul Time is the most important tool in the Toolbox for giving your child the emotional connection he desperately wants and for increasing your child's feeling of belonging and significance. It's also the most effective means of reducing negative attention-seeking behaviors."

How To Talk So Kids Will Listen & Listen So Kids Will Talk by Adele Faber & Elaine Mazlish. I particularly like Chapter 1, *Helping Children Deal with Their Feelings*, which is comparable to Chapter 6 in this book: "Acknowledge Negative Feelings. The authors involve the readers in an exercise to imagine how they would feel if their feelings were not acknowledged, but denied when they tried to express them – a good exercise to learn how children feel when their feelings are denied or dismissed. On page 33 they write, "We found that when we accepted our children's feelings they were more able to accept the limits we set for them."

Siblings Without Rivalry. Another book by Adele Faber & Elaine Mazlish. The entire book is about dealing with conflicts between siblings. There is a statement on page 204 that I like: "Kids need a lot of experiences having good times together so that when the conflicts and fights come – as they must – they both have the memory of a positive relationship they want to get back to."

350 Questions Parents Should Ask During Family Night by Shannon Alder. The author offers thought-provoking questions that parents can use to prepare their children to survive and thrive in a perilous world. This question was on page 83: "A couple of your friends are going to a party on Friday night. You just found out that you have to work that night. Your friends tell you to call in sick. What should you do?" The questions are divided into age-specific sections and are ideal for family discussions. She also provides a list of parental resources and cell phone apps.

How to Make More Money Babysitting by Kayanne Malin. A good book to give to your children to prepare them to be good babysitters. This is also a good book to give to your babysitters. It contains what parents want their babysitters to know. Subjects include: How to get customers to hire you more often, how to build self-confidence, 50 activities to keep kids busy and out of trouble, and guidelines to keep kids safe. Full disclosure: Kayanne is my oldest child and we wrote the book together.

www.ingramcontent.com/pod-product-compliance
Lightning Source LLC
Chambersburg PA
CBHW061428040426
42450CB00007B/950